Methuen Playscripts

The Methuen Playscripts series exists to extend the range of plays in print by publishing work which is not yet widely known but which has already earned a place in the acting repertoire of the modern theatre.

The Stirrings in Sheffield on Saturday Night

This 'musical documentary' was first presented at the Sheffield Playhouse Theatre in 1966, revived there in 1968, and mounted again in 1973 at the new Crucible Theatre. Against a background of Music Hall, revue sketch, monologue and folk-song, the play chronicles the violent stirrings in the Sheffield politics of the 1860s. The central problems then, as now, were wages and prices: the unions fighting the small employer and the machine; a new business attempting to compete with a monopoly. This edition contains a foreword by John Hodgson and introductions by the author, Alan Cullen, and the director, Colin George, which describe the genesis of the show and the reasons for its continued success.

D1421731

THE STIRRINGS IN SHEFFIELD ON SATURDAY NIGHT

ALAN CULLEN

Introductions by Alan Cullen and Colin George

Foreword by John Hodgson

First published in Great Britain 1974
by Eyre Methuen Ltd
11 New Fetter Lane, London EC4P 4EE
Copyright © 1974 Alan Cullen
Foreword © 1974 John Hodgson
Author's Introduction © 1974 Alan Cullen
Director's Introduction © 1974 Colin George
Music © 1974 Roderick Horn

Set by Expression Typesetters
Printed in Great Britain by
Fletcher & Son Ltd, Norwich

ISBN 0 413 31330 1 (Hardback)
ISBN 0 413 31340 9 (Paperback)

CAUTION
All rights whatsoever in this play are strictly reserved and application for
performance etc should be made before rehearsal to Green and Underwood,
11 Garrick Street, London WC2. No performance may be given unless a
licence has been obtained.

Foreword

A good many factors have contributed to the continuing success of, and interest in, *The Stirrings in Sheffield on Saturday Night*. Not least, of course, is the fact that it is a lively and entertaining piece of theatre with humour, drama, melodrama, music and music hall, all skilfully blended into an effective unity. It began as a local documentary, but it retains both a universal and an immediate appeal.

Stirrings is a documentary in the sense that its action draws on a definite basis of fact found in available first-hand historical documents. Though when the play was first produced documentary style was still something of a theatrical novelty, it has its roots in earlier drama and draws on traditions which were being established on the Continent during the first thirty years of this century. Dissatisfaction about themes and their treatment in the arts was growing. Shaw and other writers at the end of the nineteenth century aimed to make theatre more relevant and, through the fictions of playwriting, explored themes of social and moral consequence. Men like Piscator and Brecht believed that theatre did not always need to be truth embodied in escapist fantasy; facts and truths they showed might also be presented in a direct and dramatic way. These and other pioneers experimented with the idea of a living newspaper in which items of national and local significance were presented with the same immediacy that one might find in the daily press. Developments in technology gave scope for the use of slide, film and recorded sound, but at the same time they harked back to one of the oldest yet most immediate devices of them all — the use of statement through music and song. Similarly, approaches to documentary material on film, radio and television have helped to free our thinking from more conventional staging and structure. So *Stirrings*, consciously or otherwise, draws on an already established documentary tradition.

Another point of its success is that it grows out of a region and takes local history as its material. For Sheffield audiences it became 'our' play, 'our' story. Some workers in educational drama had already sensed the value of local events and characters as the focus for drama work, but it was left to Peter Cheeseman at the Victoria Theatre, Stoke-on-Trent, to pioneer this in the professional theatre. Time has led him into the belief that there is a 'story in all of us'. Within everyone's involvement with the rough and tumble of life, he feels there is material which can be shaped into 'our' drama. Of course, the more the story is in touch with the core of things, the more it transcends the local and reaches to the universal. *Stirrings* is such a piece.

But there are problems and pitfalls. When you are dealing with local matters and material of the past, when you are using song and comedy, it is also possible to by-pass immediacy and appeal simply to nostalgia. The entertainment can cloud opportunities for thinking about relevance and invite audiences to wallow in sentiment and a desire for the 'good old days'. To some extent this is certainly what happened at early performances of Joan Littlewood's prototype, *Oh, What a Lovely War*. A lot of old folk who remembered the First World War, its events and its characters, went to the theatre to enjoy once more the songs and the camaraderie, forgetting, it seemed, the irony of the title. Through the music they seemed really to believe that it was 'a lovely war'.

Stirrings is a play you can sit back to enjoy. It has all the potential to consolidate local feeling, to rekindle local pride and make one feel that at least in those days things happened in Sheffield. But it can also be a harder hitting, more thought provoking piece about universal prejudice, labour relations and civic responsibility. And what can be more immediate than that!

Bretton Hall   *John Hodgson*
1973

Author's Introduction

Plays with a documentary style of approach mostly seem to have germinated from the success of *Oh, What a Lovely War*. I cannot deny that the appeal of that show had something to do with our decision at Sheffield in the later part of 1965 to create something on those lines. Something strongly based on well-documented historical fact, presented with the minimum of obvious comment, and liberally helped out with appropriate popular songs of the period.

There, I think, the resemblance ends. A happy characteristic of the genre is that each company in tackling it has plenty of scope to develop its own variant of it. This I like to think we did with *Stirrings*. For one thing, the 'book' is not as much of a cooperative exercise as many scripts of shows of this kind tend to be; that is, the cast themselves were not asked to research and build up their own sections of it, but were presented with a complete script at the first rehearsal - just. The latter pages of it were still being duplicated as the first were being used for the reading.

The substance of the play is taken very closely from two sources - the official record of the Court of Inquiry into industrial outrages in Sheffield and Manchester in the 1860s, and newspaper reports of the time. It is worth recalling that when a show based on local history was first mooted, the general reaction of local people was 'Oh, but nothing's ever happened here . . . ', which leads one to speculate that the ultimate success of the play may be due in large part to the fascination ordinary citizens were able to find in the realization of their own antecedents. And few more so than the members of the trade unions of the town, in spite of the fact that the methods adopted by the union officials of the old days were frequently anything but admirable, and that the anti-hero, William Broadhead, was a ruthless fanatic with murder on his hands. But then, villains and their downfall have always been popular themes in the theatre.

The songs and ballads used in *Stirrings* are for the most part authentic, and local to the area. The early and mid-nineteenth century was a period rich in folk-song and ballad, especially in industrial centres. Few of the original tunes remain on record, so that new settings had to be devised, and the composer, Roderick Horn, found that the simple vigour and unaffected humanity of the words lent themselves readily to effectively theatrical instrumentation on stage via the guitar, banjo and auto-harp, producing a 'folk' sound very apt to the period. Two of the lyrics are not authentic - 'Ah Progress!' and 'Ordinary Sheffield Workmen': these were devised by John Hainsworth, who also assisted with research.

For the rest, the responsibility must be shared between myself and Colin George, the Director of the old Playhouse at Sheffield, now replaced by the larger and lusher Crucible Theatre. It should be noted that the play was originally devised for a specific company of players, with particular actors in mind from the outset. This, with the intensely local content of the material, made it a show deliberately intended for a particular community at a particular time. If it has any wider appeal - and the very fact that its subject is trades-unionism may encourage this - that was in no way the intention at the start. The primary responsibility of the Regional Theatre is to the region it serves. Much of the dialogue, therefore, is in the local idiom of the West Riding of Yorkshire, and necessarily so. At the time of writing, the play remains a favourite with the audience it was intended for, the people in and around Sheffield. Transference to the thrust stage of the Crucible from the proscenium-bound setting of the old Playhouse has presented very few problems, perhaps because the play was always conceived in a rather 'open' fashion, with minimal settings and no curtain.

Stirrings makes no attempt to take sides, or to make any particular social comment, only to show the attitudes of some of the people of the time to the events they were caught up in. We are all both the products and the authors of the course of events; the business of the documentary method is to show the events, as much as possible without hindsight, and to leave their implications to be deduced from them. William Broadhead and his associates are shown, in the main, objectively, and not, I hope, judged in any way. A psychological study of him might be interesting, but it would be a different play.

The trades union movement has grown since those days in influence and social responsibility - at least they don't blow each other up with gunpowder now - but when the union leaders of today appear on the television screen, it is not difficult to see in them the lineal descendants of William Broadhead, with many of the same feelings and motivations which made him do the things he did.

Islington   *Alan Cullen*
1973

Director's Introduction

In the Summer of 1965 I was driving over the Pennines to Sheffield from Stoke-on-Trent. I had just seen a production there at the Victoria Theatre, called *The Jolly Potters*. It had played to a large audience, a jolly audience, and one that had most certainly come from the Potteries. Peter Cheeseman, cued perhaps by *Oh, What A Lovely War*, had explored with his Company the past history of the district in which their theatre stood, and come up with a show that spoke to those living in the locality. It also had that rare quality of saying something significant in a thoroughly entertaining manner.

I had just been appointed the Director of the Sheffield Playhouse. It was a difficult time: the old regular audiences were getting increasingly frustrated by changes in theatrical taste, and resenting the substitution of the kitchen sink for the french window. A younger audience eager for contemporary modern work was unable to support us in the numbers which made running the theatre economically viable. A *Jolly Cutlers* might be a useful addition to our repertoire, I thought, as the myriad lights of Sheffield flickered into sight below. And so it proved.

We were fortunate in having a resident playwright, and I don't mean someone locked away in a room beyond the administrative offices with a typewriter, black coffee, reams of blank paper, and not an idea in sight. Alan Cullen, a schoolmaster before becoming a professional actor, had provided Sheffield Playhouse with four successful Christmas productions, and was now a member of the Company. He was giving his Fortinbras, Colonel Chesney, Roebuck Ramsden, Orsino, and David Bliss in *Hay Fever*. At the same time he had written and acted in the Christmas show - *Trudi and the Minstrel*. In that production his talents had been combined with those of Roderick Horn, another member of the Company with a flair for composing music that was eminently singable and had a real sense of period.

The idea of a musical about Sheffield was put to them. John Hainsworth, a keen supporter of the theatre working at the University, offered some research he had done on a Sheffield trade union leader of the 1860s - William Broadhead. Alan took that work further and then provided a series of scenes, Roderick set to music a number of contemporary ballads, John Hainsworth himself wrote a couple of lyrics and their combined efforts were moulded together. The links between Alan's sharp and effective episodes gave plenty of scope for the Company and director to shape and give life to the production in rehearsal. *The Stirrings* owes much to the inspiration and ingenuity of the actors, designers, and indeed the staff who have been involved in the production from the outset.

There are two stories in the play, the first dealing with the activities of William Broadhead, the saw-grinders leader in the 1860s. At that time the unions were not recognized in law, and the only way they could coerce their members into paying their dues was by intimidation or physical violence. It was a worrying time for the unions. Automation was raising its head in the cutlery trade: a machine could take over the work done formerly by a roomful of men, and some employers (the 'little mesters') were often unscrupulous in taking on too many apprentices to do the work of fully-fledged union members. Broadhead, with the connivance of the union committee, used his own methods to discipline both the grinders themselves and the small employers. The second story concerns Isaac Ironside who formed the Consumers Gas Company to compete with the already established United Gas Company which was charging, in his opinion, too much for its product. It all ended with the amalgamation of the two Companies by order of the Government. But the combined Gas Company did brings its prices down, and Ironside went off to throw his enthusiasm into other aspects of civic endeavour such as sewerage.

Stirrings opened on May 6th, 1966; it was revived that autumn, in the winter of 1968, and again in the summer of 1973. It has played virtually to capacity business since the first night, and there is something about the sheer theatrical impact of the play which is indestructible. It has survived innumerable changes of cast, and has weathered the 'sea-change' from a small proscenium theatre to the open stage of the Crucible where 1,040 spectators, within fifty-nine feet of the centre of the stage, practically surround the acting area. The basic story of a group of men achieving by violence recognition for their views within a community has become tragically more topical. *Stirrings*, however, owes its lasting popularity not to the political implications of its theme, but to an infectious and con-tinuously diverting mixture of elements in 'popular' entertainment - the variety sketch, the monologue, and, of course, the Music Hall.

Since it opened it has become a part of local history: there is even a restaurant, 'The Stirrings', named after the production. While acknowledging the contribution of those artistically involved, its success confirmed a hunch that cutlers, like potters (and no doubt like butchers, bakers and candlestick-makers) can provide an audience for the theatre - and most surely when in subject matter and treatment we meet them more than half-way.

Crucible Theatre   *Colin George*
August 1973

THE STIRRINGS IN SHEFFIELD ON SATURDAY NIGHT was first presented at The Playhouse, Sheffield, on 31 May 1966 with the following cast:

SINGERS	Roderick Horn, Dorothy Vernon
WILLIAM BROADHEAD	Wilfred Harrison
MRS BROWN	Valery Edeling
MRS FEARNEHOUGH	
MR BROWN	
FIRST WORKMAN	John Hartley
MR FEARNEHOUGH	
JAMES LINLEY	
DRUNK	
CHAIRMAN OF THE INQUIRY	Barrie Smith
CHAIRMAN OF THE MUSIC HALL	
SAMUEL CROOKES	Christopher Wilkinson
ISAAC IRONSIDE	Brian Harrison
WILLIAM LENG	
MR FLINTOFF	Alan Cullen
CHIEF CONSTABLE JACKSON	
HALLAM	Anthony Douse
MAYOR	
OLD MAN	Brian Huby
SECOND WORKMAN	Matthew O'Sullivan
THIRD WORKMAN	Neil Boorman
FOURTH WORKMAN	Michael Graves
FIRST WOMAN	Myra Frances
SECOND WOMAN	Marilyn Taylerson
OTHER WOMAN	Dorothy Vernon
SINGER (MINNIE)	
GIRL	Sharon Duce
APPRENTICES, VENDORS,	Neil Boorman, Sharon Duce,
POLICEMEN, BARMAIDS,	Valery Edeling, Myra Frances,
CITIZENS, ENTERTAINERS	Michael Graves, John Hartley,
	Brian Huby, Matthew O'Sullivan,
	Barrie Smith, Marilyn Taylerson

Directed by Colin George
Settings by Edward Furby
Costumes by Sarah Morton
Music by Roderick Horn
Research and additional lyrics by John Hainsworth

The following actors and actresses have appeared in one or more of the revival productions which opened on 29 August 1966 and 27 November 1968 at the Playhouse and on 5 April 1973 and 27 August 1973 at the new Crucible Theatre:

Michael Andrews, Ray Ashcroft, Elizabeth Bell, Tim Block, Neil Boorman, David Boyce, David Bradley, Adrienne Burgess, Fanny Carby, Ann Casson, Kenneth Colley, Barry Copping, Richard Corbett, Ronald Cuncliffe, Mark Wing Davey, Geoffrey Davies, Peter Denyer, Anthony Douse, Norman Ettlinger, Dione Ewin, Caroline Findlay, Julian Forbes, Myra Frances, Alan Fredericks, Colin George, George Hagan, Meryl Hampton, Michael Harley, Wilfred Harrison, John Hartley, Frank Hatherley, Tina Heaf, Roderick Horn, Peter Ivatts, Michael J. Jackson, Claudia Jaine, Sheila Kelley, Rosemary Kingston, Paul Lally, Veronica Lang, Geoffrey Larder, James Laurenson, Gabrielle Lloyd, David MacArthur, Elizabeth Mansfield, Zibba Mays, Maggie McCarthy, Anthony Naylor, Susan O'Brian, Neil Phillips, John Pickles, Edward Poulter, David Richardson, Joanna Robbins, Michael St John, Colin Skipp, Barrie Smith, Paul Strider, Alan Thompson, Jane Tucker, Dorothy Vernon, Christopher Wilkinson, Bruce White, Richard Wordsworth, Peter Wyatt.

Illustrations
The illustrations to the text and on the back cover show scenes from the April 1973 production. All were photographed by Roger Taylor and are reproduced with his permission.

Costumes and set were designed by Tanya Moiseivitsch.

ACT ONE

Saturday night at the 'Royal George Inn. in Carver Street. Ths inn is busy with customers, presided over by WILLIAM BROADHEAD, a stocky, urbanely expansive man practised in concealing his fanatical devotion to the union cause. Among the guests are BROWN and his attractive wife, CROOKES and HALLAM sitting separately, and two or three APPRENTICES.

Outside the scene are the SINGERS. As they sing the first verse of the song*, the pub customers remain in a tableau, or mime their activity.

SINGERS: Ye muses who mount on Parnassian towers,
    Come trooping to Sheffield and help me to sing
    The time when our sons have all got out their sours,
    And relate all the joys that our Saturdays bring.
          But hard words and Greek-em
          Let learned folk speak 'em;
  It's epic and tragic, bombastic we'll write;
          And loudly we'll sing-o
          In plain English lingo
  The stirrings in Sheffield on Saturday night.

ALL (coming to life and moving): And loudly we'll sing-o
                         In plain English lingo
      The stirrings in Sheffield on Saturday night!

SINGERS: Of hammers and files now no more of their din is,
    At the door of the warehouse the workmen are ranged,
    While the masters their banknotes and smug little guineas
    Are counting and strutting about to get changed,
          Having reckoned they'd ne'er stop
          Repair to the beer-shop,
  Where the fumes of tobacco and stingo invite;
          And the oven inhabits
          A store of welsh rabbits
  To feast jovial fellows on Saturday night.

ALL: And loudly we'll sing-o
          In plain English lingo
  The stirrings in Sheffield on Saturday night.

(The scene continues with activity as the SINGERS move in among the rest for the next verse, pointing the lines of the song with reference to the customer's action.)

SINGERS: Then while Sheffield liquor around they are pushing

*Selected music for the play begins on page 89.

There's many a chorus melodious to rise -

APPRENTICES (soulfully): O Genevieve, Sweet Genevieve.

SINGERS: Though oft interrupted by merchants who rush in
With 'Cockles Alive-O' or 'Hot Mutton Pies!'

(FIRST VENDOR and SECOND VENDOR enter on cue.)

FIRST VENDOR (singing): 'Cockles Alive-O!'

SECOND VENDOR (singing): '- and Hot Mutton Pies!'

(VENDORS join the rest. SINGERS turn to a table where a man reads a
newspaper.)

SINGERS: Perhaps you may choose, sir,
        To pore o'er the news, sir,
And tell whether matters go wrong or go right -

MAN (speaking): Shocking. I tell you it's shocking. It's the bloody Government.

SINGERS: For all ranks and conditions
        Commence politicians
While sat at the alehouse on Saturday night.

ALL: And loudly we'll sing-o
          In plain English lingo
The stirrings in Sheffield on Saturday night!

(Activity continues, subdued. The SINGERS move out of the bar to a
presumed alley alongside, with LOVING COUPLE.)

SINGERS: As through the dark alleys, if slily one pops,
What fun they may hear, if an ear they will lend;
Such sighs and soft wishes from lads and from lasses
Who tell their fond tales at an entry end

BOY: Go on, Polly.

GIRL: Oh, I couldn't . . .

BOY: Please, Polly.

GIRL: You know I shouldn't.

BOY: Aye, but I know you will, though!

GIRL: Oh, you are awful.

SINGERS: Then he to his true love
        Says, 'Polly, adieu, love'
And kisses and squeezes his lassie so tight;
        And softly she'll cry, sir,
        She'll blush and say, 'Fie, sir,

GIRL: Can't you stay a bit longer - it's Saturday night!'

(The SINGERS move back into the pub.)

SINGERS: Thus with drinking and smoking
          And laughing and joking
  They put wrinkled sorrow and care to the flight
          And over the sting-o
          They laugh, chat and sing-o,
  And merrily welcome each Saturday night.

ALL: And over the sting-o
          We laugh, chat and sing-o,
  And merrily welcome each Saturday night!

BROADHEAD: Last orders, please.

MRS BROWN: Not yet, love, for crying out loud. I'm stone cold sober.

BROADHEAD: I'm sure no one in this room has ever seen you any other way, Mrs Brown.

MRS BROWN: Oh, isn't he lovely? Why do you never say things like that to me, Dicky?

BROWN: Eh?

MRS BROWN: What Mr Broadhead just said.

BROWN: What did he say?

MRS BROWN: Oh, get me another port and then jump int canal.

(LINLEY enters and goes to the bar. He is a thin-faced man of about forty, with a certain shiftiness under his geniality.)

Why, Mr Linley!

LINLEY: Now then, what'll it be, eh? What'll it be, Dicky?

BROWN: Eh?

MRS BROWN: Don't keep saying eh. You'll have the bar shut before we've got us order in. Pint for him and a small port for me, Mr Linley.

LINLEY: Let's make it a large one, shall we?

MRS BROWN: My word, we are flush tonight, aren't we?

LINLEY (jingling his money): Plenty more where that came from, love. (He turns to bar.) Two pints, and a large port for the lady.

(BROADHEAD deliberately puts the towel over the pumps.)

BROADHEAD: Time, please.

MRS BROWN: Not yet!

BROWN: Oh, no!

(Brief general protest, mechanical for the most part.)

BROADHEAD: Time, ladies and gentlemen. (Pointedly.) Good night, Mr Linley.

LINLEY: Well, I'll go to bloody hell.

(LINLEY goes out.)

BROADHEAD: Sup up, lads and lasses. We've all got to get up in t' morning, you know. Glasses, please.

MRS BROWN (as the BROWNS go out): It's all your fault, with your everlasting eh? what? I shan't sleep now for thinking about it.

(The customers drift out, the APPRENTICES singing as they go. CROOKES remains behind. BROADHEAD comes out from behind the bar, wiping his hands on a cloth.)

BROADHEAD: Well, Sam?

CROOKES: What about Linley, then?

BROADHEAD: What about him?

CROOKES: Are we to have another go at him, are we?

BROADHEAD: It's up to you.

CROOKES: Nay, you're the union secretary, Mr Broadhead.

BROADHEAD: Treasurer, Sam, only the treasurer at the moment.

CROOKES: Well, whatever it is. You give the orders, any road.

BROADHEAD: If I do, it's because nobody else will. And don't think I like doing it, because I don't. But there's certain men from time to time that have to be . . . disciplined. That's all it is - a question of discipline. There's nothing personal. A union is like an army, Sam - it has to fight for its life. And an army can't fight without discipline.

CROOKES: What do you want us to do, then?

BROADHEAD: And Linley is a man who is not amenable to ordinary discipline. When I think of the damage he does to the trade, when I think of the way he flouts the union rules, it makes my heart bleed for all those good, conscientious members who have to suffer because of a few renegades like Linley. I tell you, Sam, it makes my heart bleed.

CROOKES: . . . We've blown his house up with gunpowder once, and shot him.

BROADHEAD: He's got to be stopped one way or another. Stopped from taking on more lads than he should do, stopped from paying under union rates, stopped from turning out bad work. His own lads had to duck him in t' trough not long since, before he'd pay 'em the miserable money they do get. I want him made so he can't work, so he can't carry on in defiance of union rules!

CROOKES: I'll make sure he doesn't work any more . . . . He'll not get away with it this time.

BROADHEAD: But there's one thing I want to make quite clear to you, Sam. He's not to be killed. I won't have him killed. We're not murderers. Just make him so he'll never work again. That's all. Just so he never works again.

(Sings 'The Grinders' Hardships'.)

To be a Sheffield grinder, it is no easy trade.
There's more than you'd imagine in the grinding of a blade.
The strongest man among us is old at thirty-two,
For there's few who brave the hardships that we poor grinders do.

WORKMEN (entering): When the country goes to war, then our masters
   quickly cry,
   'Orders countermanded', our goods we all lay by;
   Our prices we must settle, and you'll be stinted too -
   There's few suffer such hardships as we poor grinders do.

   And every working day we are breathing dust and steel,
   And a broken stone can give us a wound that will not heal,
   There's many a honest grinder ground down by such a blow,
   For there's few that brave such hardships as we poor grinders do.

   There's many a poor grinder who's thus been snatched away
   Without a moment's warning to meet the Judgement Day;
   Before his Judge he must appear, his final doom to know -
   There are few who brave such hardships as we poor grinders do.

   Thus many a poor grinder whose family is large
   Without his best endeavours cannot his debts discharge,
   When children cry for bread, how pitiful the view,
   Though few can brave such hardships as we poor grinders do.

   And now I will conclude these few and humble lines
   With 'Success To All Grinders' who suffer in hard times;
   I wish them better fortune and all their families too,
   There are few who brave such hardships as we poor grinders do.

A Sheffield street at night, dimly illuminated by a bracketed gas-lamp at the corner. The voice of ISAAC IRONSIDE booms from the darkness before he appears.

IRONSIDE (off): Filth, Mr Flintoff, filth.

   (IRONSIDE enters with FLINTOFF, an erstwhile London bookseller.)

   Whilst there is darkness, there will be filth. Whilst there is darkness, there will be corruption, immorality, and crime. Where there is light, there is cleanliness and order. We must give the people light.

FLINTOFF: The darkness you speak of is the darkness of the mind, I take it, Mr Ironside.

IRONSIDE: The darkness I speak of is the darkness of the streets, Mr Flintoff.

(A PROSTITUTE crosses the street.)

FLINTOFF: Oh. Well, yes, one certainly faces certain hazards in negotiating the poorer parts of the town, it's true.

IRONSIDE: I am not thinking of my own comfort, nor of yours. I am thinking of the moral and physical welfare of the ordinary citizen of this town. Light, Mr Flintoff, light must be brought into these dark places; not for my good, nor for your good, but for the good of struggling humanity.

FLINTOFF: You are absolutely right, of course, but what's the answer?

IRONSIDE: The answer, my dear sir, is gas.

FLINTOFF: Gas?

IRONSIDE: Gas.

FLINTOFF: But we have gas.

IRONSIDE: I have gas. You have gas. But does every humble family in this city have gas? No, it does not. And why not? Because that precious commodity costs twice the amount in Sheffield that it does in London, whereas the coal from which it comes costs half as much.

FLINTOFF: Half as much?

IRONSIDE: Half as much. Think of that.

FLINTOFF: Oh, I am thinking of it.

IRONSIDE: Well?

FLINTOFF: Well what?

IRONSIDE: What is the obvious conclusion?

FLINTOFF: That when it comes to filth, Sheffield has it over London?

IRONSIDE: Not exactly, Mr Flintoff. Let me put it another way. How can we remedy this insupportable state of affairs?

FLINTOFF: More gas?

IRONSIDE: Well, yes, more gas of course; but they can't afford it.

FLINTOFF: No. More wages?

IRONSIDE: What, to be squandered in the alehouse?

FLINTOFF: No, of course not. How foolish of me. Cheaper gas?

IRONSIDE: Ah.

FLINTOFF: Of course. I don't know why I didn't think of it at first.

IRONSIDE: Cheaper gas, Mr Flintoff. I shall not rest until every Sheffield cottage is lit by gas - and lit for tuppence a week.

FLINTOFF: Tuppence a week!

IRONSIDE: Tuppence a week. And not only that; every street shall be lit with gas of a reasonable price and fair illuminative power, as the most effective means of keeping down that flood of public immorality which I and every man of principle can only deplore.

FLINTOFF: Deplore, yes. You speak extremely well, Councillor Ironside.

IRONSIDE: Thank you. But it is deeds, not words, that will illuminate the streets and homes of the poor, my dear sir.

FLINTOFF: True. Oh, very true. Yes. But there is a slight difficulty, if I may venture to say so.

IRONSIDE: The project bristles with difficulties; I have never yet supported a project that didn't. To what particular difficulty do you refer?

FLINTOFF: How are you to persuade the United Gas Company to reduce the price of its gas?

IRONSIDE: Competition, Mr Flintoff.

FLINTOFF: Competition?

IRONSIDE: I shall produce my own gas.

FLINTOFF: I don't quite follow.

IRONSIDE: I shall form my own gas company, to be called The Sheffield Consumers' Gas Company. It will have one purpose, and one purpose only - to serve the people. We shall supply gas at three shillings per thousand cubic feet, meters and service pipes will be supplied free of charge, and there will be a uniform price for all classes of consumer. As to capital, I propose to raise say £60,000 in £5 shares, and acquire borrowing powers for, say £100,000.

FLINTOFF: A noble scheme, Councillor. Truly a noble scheme.

IRONSIDE: And we shall launch it nobly. The foundation stone shall be laid to the thunder of cannon -

(Cannons off.)

The ringing of church bells -

(Church bells. The lights begin to come up on a bunting-draped platform upstage.)

The march of troops, the flying of colours, and the strains of the cavalry band!

(Marching feet, clattering hooves, and 'Colonel Bogey'. IRONSIDE and FLINTOFF ascend the platform where the MAYOR waits to lay the foundation stone.)

MAYOR: And it is with great pleasure, and I may say - and indeed I will say - pride; pride in the vision, in the, in the foresight, in the selfless dedication to-er-to, to civic advancement and the welfare of the people on the part of such men as Councillor, ah, Councillor Ironside, that I, ah, that I now declare this, ah, this stone, yes this stone, ah, well and truly laid.

(Cheers. Band. Cannon. Fade.)

Loud cacophony of steel ingots being struck like bells. Cheers fading down. Spot comes up on the WORKMEN.

WORKMEN: Here's a health to he that is now set free
   That once was a prentice bound.
   It is for his sake this feast we make
   And so let his health go round.

(Lights on group of MEN and APPRENTICES with beer-mugs. Renewed clanging of ingots as the LAD is lifted up on two men's shoulders to a cheer.)

Hold your liquor above your chin.

(A mug of ale is handed up to the LAD. Rest of the verse as he holds the mugs above his face, preparing to pour the liquor at one go down his throat.)

Open your mouth and let liquor run in.

(The LAD attempts to pour the liquor down his throat.)

LINLEY: I'll hold you a crown it's all gone down.

(He finishes the ale. Cheers.)

WORKMEN: Here's a health to he that is now set free.

(The LAD is carried round, as they all sing the refrain. The group dissolves. LINLEY detaches himself from the rest. The LAD is let down and comes forward to meet LINLEY as the rest disappear.)

LINLEY: How does it feel to be out of your time, then?

LAD: I don't know. It's a bit like being twenty-one, or having a woman for t' first time - you think you should feel different, but you don't.

LINLEY: Well, you're a bright enough lad. You'll do all right for yourself, I should think.

LAD: Will I? Happen I will if I don't let on I was one of Linley's lads.

LINLEY: What? That's a nice thing to say, isn't it? After I've taught you everything you know?

LAD: Well, I'm only saying -

LINLEY: And after me taking you on when you couldn't get in anywhere else? You're a fine example of the gratitude of the modern generation, aren't you?

LAD: I'm only saying your lads don't find it so easy to get work, and they don't.

LINLEY: Who says they don't?

LAD: Everybody.

LINLEY: You mean every bloody half-baked arse-creeping union man. Listen - if I took any notice of anything they said I'd be living on t' parish if I were living at all.

LAD: We've got to have unions.

LINLEY: Have we? You're a fine one to talk. If I hadn't stood up to t' union and gone my own road, you for one wouldn't have a good trade at your fingers' ends like you have this minute. Would you?

LAD: Well, I don't -

LINLEY: Would you?

LAD: Happen I wouldn't, but -

LINLEY: You know bloody well you wouldn't. Well, I'll tell you this much; no bloody alecan of a union secretary's going to lay the law down to me about how many prentices I can take on, nor nowt else. I'll tell you that.

(LINLEY breaks off, and glances over his shoulder. He continues in a lower voice.)

Aye, I'll tell you that.

LAD: What's up, Mr Linley?

LINLEY: What do you mean, what's up?

LAD: I don't know. You look scared or summat.

LINLEY: I'm scared of nobody in this town.

LAD: They're not after you again, are they?

LINLEY: They're always after me. Two goes they've had at me up to now, but they'll not stop me, not while they stop my breath in me body they won't.

LAD: Nay, they've never killed anybody as I know of.

LINLEY: Not yet they haven't . . . ey up! Who's at yon corner? Behind me?

LAD: Two men. Why?

LINLEY: One with a brown tommy liner hat on?

LAD: Aye. What about 'em?

LINLEY: Nowt. Nowt at all. Only . . . just walk along with me, will you, lad, while we get to where there's more of a crowd, like.

LAD: Aye, if you like, Mr Linley.

(They begin to move.)

Only what you were just saying about union men, you know, they're not all -

LINLEY: Talk about summat else, will you? I'm getting sick o' t' subject . . .

(They move off. CROOKES and HALLAM appear and follow them.)

HALLAM: Where do you reckon he's going now?

CROOKES: American Stores, then he'll go for a drink.

HALLAM: It's time we did him. Broadhead thinks so too.

CROOKES: There's too many folk about.

HALLAM: Well, I'm getting fed up, I'll tell you. If we don't do him today, I'm having nowt no more to do with it.

CROOKES: Oh, aye, you can afford to pass up seven pound ten any day of the week, can't you?

HALLAM: Five . . . six weeks we've been after Linley, all over Sheffield. It's cost me more nor seven quid in shoe leather. I've very near forgot what it's all about.

(CROOKES takes his air-gun from under his coat, and wipes it.)

CROOKES: You know what it's about. Linley is obnoxious to the trade.

HALLAM: Aye, I know.

CROOKES: Goes again the union and damages the trade when we can't afford to have it damaged. He's obnoxious.

HALLAM: Well, what the bloody 'ell are we waiting for, then? Come on, or else we'll lose him.

(CROOKES and HALLAM follow after LINLEY.)

A street. Two WORKMEN are digging a hole. An OLD MAN emerges from a house and watches them for a few minutes in silence. One of the WORK-MEN looks up and catches his eye.

OLD MAN: Nah then.

FIRST WORKMAN: Nah then.

(He resumes his digging. The OLD MAN regards them for a short time, then goes into the house and comes out with a chair. He places it care-fully, and settles down to watch.)

OLD MAN: It's a grand hole.

FIRST WORKMAN: Eh?

OLD MAN: I say it's a grand hole.

FIRST WORKMAN: Oh, aye.

OLD MAN: I know a good hole when I see one. I've dug some right lovely holes in my time, you know.

FIRST WORKMAN: Have you?

OLD MAN: I have an all . . . some lovely holes. Hey.

FIRST WORKMAN: What?

OLD MAN: It's a nicer hole nor what they're digging in t' next street.

FIRST WORKMAN: Is it?

OLD MAN: Oh, aye. Straighter, like, cleaner if you know what I mean. I like a good clean hole.

FIRST WORKMAN: Thanks very much.

OLD MAN: I just thought I'd tell you . . . You don't mind me watching you, do you?

FIRST WORKMAN: All t' same to me, dad.

OLD MAN: No, but there's some as does and some as doesn't. Now I didn't used to mind. Holes, you see, holes was me life. Now they're me hobby . . . Hey, I say.

FIRST WORKMAN: What?

OLD MAN: What's it, like, what's it for? I mean a hole's a hole, nobody appreciates that more nor what I do, but what are they digging all those holes for up and down? I mean what are you going to put in 'em?

FIRST WORKMAN: Gas.

OLD MAN: Ah, now then, you see, I told her. I told her it was gas. I said so - I said it was never sewerage. I said that closet, I said, it'll see my time out and yours an all. We'll never have a tipple in our time . . . Gas, eh? Have you, like, have you ever thought about gas? Have you, like, considered it at all?

FIRST WORKMAN: Not me, dad, I just dig t' holes.

OLD MAN: Aye, well, it's a wonderful thing, you know, is gas. Wonderful. All them pipes. Ramificatin'. Ramificatin' all over.

FIRST WORKMAN: They what?

OLD MAN: They ramificate.

FIRST WORKMAN: I shouldn't have thought they could.

OLD MAN: Aye, well they do. All over. Have you ever thought what it must be like, all them pipes?

FIRST WORKMAN: I can't say I have.

OLD MAN: I have. You'd start off, like, from your meter it might be, crawling through them little narrow tunnels, through all sorts of joints and junctions, getting bigger and bigger as you went further and further on till you were in t' gas main, and you'd start running and running down it, and all of a sudden there you'd be.

FIRST WORKMAN: Where?

OLD MAN: There. In t' gasholder. All big, and empty and quiet and dark - like being in a cathedral . . . It's a wonderful thing is gas.

VOICE (off): Josiah.

OLD MAN: Hello.

VOICE: Your dinner's out.

OLD MAN: I'm coming. Aye, wonderful it is, wonderful. (Picks up chair.) Ta-ra, then. It's been very interesting talking to you - very interesting indeed.

FIRST WORKMAN: Hey, dad.

OLD MAN: What?

FIRST WORKMAN: Is there a boozer round here, is there?

OLD MAN: Round t' corner. 'Grinders' Arms'. See you this afternoon.

(The OLD MAN goes in.)

FIRST WORKMAN: Come on, we'll have a quick 'un.

SECOND WORKMAN: What if t' foreman comes round?

FIRST WORKMAN: He'll more likely to be there himself. Come on.

(The WORKMEN go off. Immediately, TWO OTHER WORKMEN appear, with shovels.)

THIRD WORKMAN: This'll be it.

FOURTH WORKMAN: Are you sure?

THIRD WORKMAN: It's Trafalgar Street, int it?

FOURTH WORKMAN: Aye, I think so.

THIRD WORKMAN: Well, then. Come on, let's fill it in.

(He starts shovelling.)

FOURTH WORKMAN: I don't know, though. It looks like one of ours.

THIRD WORKMAN: Get away. Their holes is not same as ours.

FOURTH WORKMAN: Are you sure?

THIRD WORKMAN: Course I'm sure. A United hole is superior altogether to what theirs is. There's summat about it - there's nowt about this.

FOURTH WORKMAN: I don't know, though. It's not a bad hole, you know.

THIRD WORKMAN: It's a rotten hole; look at its bottom. Would you own up to a bottom like that?

FOURTH WORKMAN: Well, no, I wouldn't. But them sides - wouldn't you say that's a George Tinsley side?

THIRD WORKMAN: That? I hope George never hears you say that's one of his sides. He'd flatten you.

FOURTH WORKMAN: It's not unlike, you know.

THIRD WORKMAN: Get off. Sides, bottom, lip and all - it's a Consumer hole if I ever saw one. Come on, or else we'll be here all bloody day.

(They continue filling. Presently, the OLD MAN comes out.)

OLD MAN: You've been sharp, haven't you?

THIRD WORKMAN: You what?

OLD MAN: I say you've been sharp.

THIRD WORKMAN: Sharp over what?

VOICE (off): Come and finish your dinner Josiah.

OLD MAN: All right I'm coming.

(The OLD MAN goes in.)

THIRD WORKMAN: What's up with him?

FOURTH WORKMAN: He's what they call senile. Me grandad's same, only they keep him locked up.

(The OLD MAN hurries out again with his chair and the rest of his dinner.)

THIRD WORKMAN: Tha doesn't miss much, does tha?

OLD MAN: No, well, it's a quiet street, you see; we don't have much excitement here . . . Hey!

FOURTH WORKMAN: What's up now?

OLD MAN: You're fillin' it in.

FOURTH WORKMAN: Aye, that's right.

OLD MAN: I mean, you've only just dug it.

THIRD WORKMAN: Oh no we ain't. This 'ere's a Consumer hole; we're United men, us.

OLD MAN: I *thought* you weren't same; I said to her, I said -

THIRD WORKMAN: What the bloody 'ell's it got to do with thee, any road?

OLD MAN: Eh?

THIRD WORKMAN: Thee get thy rice puddin' eaten and mind thy own bloody business. Come on, let's get done.

(The WORKMEN fill the hole in silence. The OLD MAN, crushed, watches them for a few minutes, then picks up his chair and goes to his door.)

OLD MAN: There'll be some fun when t' other lot comes back, all t' same. They're bigger nor you two, you know.

(He goes in.)

FOURTH WORKMAN: Daft old devil. Hey, I wonder if they are.

THIRD WORKMAN: What?

FOURTH WORKMAN: Bigger than us.

THIRD WORKMAN: Don't be so daft. What can they do?

(They look at each other, then shovel furiously, stamp the earth down, and pause.)

Well, what are we waiting for?

(They shoulder their shovels and move away. The FIRST and SECOND WORKMEN reappear and take in the situation.)

FIRST WORKMAN: Well, I'll go to my - Hey!

THIRD WORKMAN: You talking to me?

FIRST WORKMAN: Well, I'm not talking to thy bloody shovel. What do you think you're on, eh?

THIRD WORKMAN: What do you mean, what do I think I'm on?

FIRST WORKMAN: What about this here hole?

THIRD WORKMAN: What about it?

FIRST WORKMAN: Tha knows well enough what about it. Well, tha can just open it up again, that's what.

(The OLD MAN has meantime reappeared, eagerly interested.)

THIRD WORKMAN: Oh, I can, can I?

FIRST WORKMAN: Tha can that, or else I'll open up thee - wi' this.

(He raises his shovel.)

OLD MAN: I told her there'd be some fun - I told her.

THIRD WOMAN: Listen, I'll tell thee summat. If I did dig it out again for thee, it'd be a damn sight better than it were afore.

FIRST WORKMAN: Tha what?

THIRD WORKMAN: I'm telling thee - I wouldn't be found dead in a hole like that.

FIRST WORKMAN: Why, you cheeky - !

(FIRST WORKMAN attacks THIRD WORKMAN with his shovel. The other two join in. The OLD MAN has meanwhile brought out his chair and another plateful of rice pudding, and is eagerly watching and eating.)

OLD MAN: Up the Consumers! Up the New Gas Company! Go on, lads - let 'em have it! - you're winning - you're winning - OH!

(The FOURTH WORKMAN has laid out the SECOND WORKMAN.)

Up the United!

(The FIRST lays out the FOURTH.)

Up the Consumers!

(The THIRD lays out the FIRST.)

Up the -

(The FIRST WORKMAN turns to the OLD MAN.)

United . . . ?

(The OLD MAN grabs his chair and scuttles indoors. IRONSIDE appears with FLINTOFF.)

IRONSIDE: Well, how goes the great work, my lad?

THIRD WORKMAN: Piss off!

(The THIRD WORKMAN totters away. IRONSIDE and FLINTOFF look blankly at each other. SINGERS enter and all join in 'The Progress Song'.)

SINGERS: Though coal was cheap in Sheffield
             And labour costs were small,
             The price of gas was twice as much
             As anywhere else at all.

WORKMEN (sing chorus): Oh, Progress!
             This favour we entreat:
             Get beautiful big gasometers built
             In every Sheffield street!

SINGERS: The cause of this anomoly
             Was easy to remark,
             'Twas the rich man's greed for profit
             Kept the poor folk in the dark.

             (Chorus.)

             A champion of progress
             Rose up to set things right.
             He vowed that those in darkness
             Should soon have cheaper light.

             (Chorus.)

             Then darkness would be scattered
             And dirt be washed away,
             And vice have nowhere left to hide
             Upon that golden day.

             (Chorus.)

             Though coal was cheap in Sheffield
             And labour costs were small,
             The price of gas was twice as much
             As anywhere else at all.

             (Chorus.)

FIRST WOMAN - RUBY - is behind bar. FLINTOFF sits at a public house table reading a newspaper. LINLEY enters and goes to them.

LINLEY: Nah then.

FLINTOFF: Mr Linley isn't it?

LINLEY: Will you join me?

FLINTOFF: No thank you.

LINLEY: Pint of ale, Ruby.

(RUBY draws the ale.)

FLINTOFF: We don't often see you in here.

LINLEY: No, well I shift my ground a bit these days.

FLINTOFF: How's that arm of yours?

LINLEY: That's eighteen months or more since. Take more than a slug in the arm to keep me down.

FLINTOFF: Or a bottle of gunpowder either, eh?

LINLEY: Just shows you what they are.

FLINTOFF: Have you any idea who did it?

LINLEY: Some poor sod doing their dirty work for 'em. There's plenty as could do with a few pound for slipping a canful of gunpowder down your chimney. You try to go your own road and you're obnoxious to them. That's what they call you - obnoxious to the trade. So they ratten you. And if rattening doesn't work, they try summat worse. There's nothing more filthy than sneaking up to a man's home in t' middle o' t' night with a can of gunpowder. Doesn't matter to them if his wife and kids are there too, oh no - they have to earn their miserable blood money. But I don't blame them as much as them as sets 'em on to it - like that bloody hypocrite in Carver Street.

FLINTOFF: Who's that? You mean Mr Broadhead?

LINLEY: Who else would I mean?

FLINTOFF: How should I know? I'm not in the trade.

LINLEY: You know all right. So does everybody, but they keep their mouths shut.

FLINTOFF: Everybody doesn't go looking for trouble either.

LINLEY: Do I look for trouble, then?

FLINTOFF: I don't know, but it does have a habit of tagging on after you, doesn't it?

LINLEY: Listen. All I want 'em to do is to leave me alone. How's that looking for trouble? All I want 'em to do is to stop bloody interfering and let me go my own road.

FLINTOFF: I know, but if you're going to make a trade union work, you have to have everybody keeping to t' rules, it's only common sense.

LINLEY: And what if you don't agree with their rules? Are you to starve then?

FLINTOFF: I know it's hard, but you've got to give in a bit now and again for the good of everybody. The unions do good, you know.

LINLEY: They've never done nowt for me. I've never had a penny out o' t' box in my life.

FLINTOFF: There's many a man would be starving if it weren't for the union box, all the same.

LINLEY: All right. So they look after them as hasn't enough to look after theirselves, and they stand up to t' masters now and again, I'm not saying they don't, but that doesn't give 'em no right to act like they was God Almighty, like Owd Smeetem up yonder.

FLINTOFF: Well, I don't know that I agree with everything they do, but as long as the law doesn't recognize the existence of the trade unions, it's not surprising they make their own laws, is it?

LINLEY: Come here and I'll tell you summat.

(LINLEY leans forward and talks in a low voice. HALLAM and CROOKES appear. They are in the alleyway between the pub and the next building. There is, or is presumed to be, a window between LINLEY and them. BROWN and MRS BROWN enter the snug.)

MRS BROWN: Why, look who's here!

BROWN: Eh?

MRS BROWN: If it isn't Mr Linley.

LINLEY (rising): Ah, the fair Mrs Brown. Mr Brown.

BROWN (none too pleased): Linley.

LINLEY: How about that drink, then? Will you join me?

MRS BROWN: Never say no, Mr Linley. I'll have a small port.

LINLEY: Dicky?

BROWN: Eh? Oh—er—no, no thank you. I just want a word with - er - excuse me.

(BROWN escapes from them and goes out.)

LINLEY: What have I done now?

MRS BROWN: Oh, pay no attention to him, he's in one of his moods.

LINLEY (to RUBY): Same again and a small port . . . Business bad, then?

MRS BROWN: I'm sure I don't know. Just how many houses he sells is no affair of mine. You don't seem to do so badly.

LINLEY: Oh, I manage. I'm not thinking of emigrating yet, any road.

FLINTOFF: Plenty over here are giving it very serious consideration lately.

MRS BROWN: What do people want to emigrate for, any road?

FLINTOFF: There's opportunities over in America.

MRS BROWN: I've all the opportunities I want here thank you. (Taking a glass from RUBY.) Your health.

FLINTOFF: All men free and equal. They say.

MRS BROWN: They're free enough on this side of the Atlantic if you ask me.

LINLEY: There's opportunities, I know, and there's free education and there's democracy, more than what we've got 'ere, but there's big trouble brewing up over yonder, specially int South. There'll be a war any time.

MRS BROWN: Oh well, if you're going to talk politics, I may as well go back to my husband. Thanks for the port, Mr Linley.

LINLEY: Have another.

MRS BROWN: Ee, I daren't. Not with him in one of his moods. Jealous, you know. Very jealous. Enjoy yourselves.

(MRS BROWN leaves them and goes out of the snug. LINLEY leans over to FLINTOFF, and they continue talking in a low voice. Attention switches to CROOKES and HALLAM in the alleyway outside.)

HALLAM: She's gone!

CROOKES: Ay.

HALLAM: He's talking to Flintoff.

CROOKES: Foxy bugger. He knows he's safe when there's other folk round him.

HALLAM: Look, he's leant down. You can get him easy - just here in't shoulder.

CROOKES: I might hit somebody else - I might hit Flintoff.

HALLAM: You can't miss him man.

CROOKES: Which road can we run? Is there anybody down yonder?

HALLAM: I can't see nobody. We can get out through Peacroft - are you going to do him or not?

CROOKES: It's too risky. We'll - just a minute Flintoff's going. He's on his own now.

HALLAM: If you don't bloody do him now, I'll do you. You'll never have a better chance, I'm telling you. Get him. Get him *now*.

(CROOKES shoots. There is the thud of an air-gun and the crash of glass. LINLEY rises, his hands to his head.)

CROOKES: I've hit him. I've hit him in t' head.

(LINLEY falls, as FLINTOFF springs to his feet.)

HALLAM: Come on. Come on for Christ's sake!

CROOKES: By God, I think I've killed him.

HALLAM (drags CROOKES away): For Christ's sake, run!

(They run down the alley, as pub customers converge on LINLEY, and the light fades. SINGERS enter and WORKMEN join in the song 'We're Ordinary Sheffield Workmen'.)

SINGERS and WORKMEN: We're ordinary Sheffield workmen
And we don't want to kill,
But we have wives and children
And they have bellies to fill.

Bill Broadhead kept the Royal George,
It stands in Carver Street,
And there for recreation
The Sheffield grinders meet.

Bill Broadhead was their leader,
And whatever duty fell,
You could be sure Bill Broadhead
Would serve his union well.

It was a time of hardship
When jobs were very few,
But when a man was out of work
Bill Broadhead saw him through.

We're ordinary Sheffield workmen
And we don't want to kill,
But we have wives and children
And they have bellies to fill.

James Linley was a grinder
Who ground inferior saws.
He undercut the proper rates
And broke the Union laws.

He kept too many apprentices
And when they'd learnt their trade,
He turned them out and left them
To live off Union aid.

He got a warning letter,
It was signed by Mary Ann.
Bill Broadhead sent it to him,
But he never gave a damn.

We're ordinary Sheffield workmen
And we don't want to kill,
But we have wives and children
And they have bellies to fill.

Bill Broadhead sent for Hallam
And sent for Crookes also -
Two out-of-work saw-grinders:
They knew what they must do.

These men began to follow
Wherever Linley fled.
They caught him in a tavern
And shot him in the head.

We're ordinary Sheffield workmen
And we don't want to kill,
But we have wives and children
And they have bellies to fill.

A WOMAN is sweeping her front doorstep. A SECOND WOMAN passes and stops.

FIRST WOMAN: Hello, love. How are you anyway?

SECOND WOMAN: Oh, I'm as well as can be expected.

FIRST WOMAN: Men. You want to turn your back on him a bit oftener.

SECOND WOMAN: Oh, he's not so bad. He turns his wages over regular. I'll say that.

FIRST WOMAN: All of it?

SECOND WOMAN: Well, most of what's left after he's paid the union his natty.

FIRST WOMAN: How do you know? How do you know what he gets? Has he ever told you?

SECOND WOMAN: I wouldn't ask him. It's a man's privilege.

FIRST WOMAN: Aye, that's what they all say.

SECOND WOMAN: Well, it is. I wouldn't think so much of a man as told his wife everything.

FIRST WOMAN: When's it due.

SECOND WOMAN: November - I think.

FIRST WOMAN: Don't you know?

SECOND WOMAN: I've never been so good at reckoning up.

FIRST WOMAN: And then they talk about giving women votes.

SECOND WOMAN: Votes?

FIRST WOMAN: Some folk think it's time everybody voted - women an' all.

SECOND WOMAN: Nay, they'll never do that. I don't think I'd like it, any road. I'd rather leave it to Walter.

FIRST WOMAN: Well, I think it's time women took a hand in things. Things could be a lot different if they did.

SECOND WOMAN: Oh? What would you do?

FIRST WOMAN: I'd shut half o' the alehouses for a start. That's where most of their brass goes.

SECOND WOMAN: Oh, I don't know. It's dry work, you know. I think a man's entitled -

FIRST WOMAN: A man's entitled to put plenty in his kids' bellies afore he fills his own with liquor. I've no patience. And I'd stop all this union caper an' all. Your Walter's union's on strike now - fork-grinders - and they're fetching extra police in, as if we hadn't enough already. They're like a lot of bloody school kids.

SECOND WOMAN: Walter says unions have been the salvation of the working man.

FIRST WOMAN: What? Salvation? Well, if he thinks blowing folks up int middle o' t' night and tracking 'em down and shooting 'em like animals is salvation, he's a funny idea of being saved, that's all I can say.

SECOND WOMAN: Why, who's been shot?

FIRST WOMAN: How do I know — Hindley or Linley or summat - it's all in the Independent. They shot him, any road, because he wouldn't knuckle under to t' union men.

SECOND WOMAN: I thought that chap Brown did it.

FIRST WOMAN: It's only police as thinks so. Everybody else knows t' union were at back of it. That's their road of doing things. They make me sick.

SECOND WOMAN: Well I don't know anything about them things and I don't want to know. I'd rather leave it to Walter.

FIRST WOMAN: Aye. How many have you now?

SECOND WOMAN: What?

FIRST WOMAN: Bairns.

SECOND WOMAN: Oh, this is only my third. We lost the first two with the croup.

FIRST WOMAN: Never mind, love, you've plenty of time yet. Just leave it to Walter.

The 'Royal George'. CROOKES enters. To him, BROADHEAD, in shirt sleeves, wiping his hands.

BROADHEAD: Are you by yourself?

CROOKES: Aye.

BROADHEAD: Where's Hallam?

CROOKES: Downstairs.

BROADHEAD: Oh.

CROOKES: I reckon you know what we've come for.

BROADHEAD: Yes. You've done well.

CROOKES: We did what we agreed we would do.

   (BROADHEAD takes out a cash-box and counts out money.)

   What's this?

BROADHEAD: Twelve pound.

CROOKES: Twelve? We were to have fifteen for this job.

BROADHEAD: Well?

CROOKES: Well, what about the other three.

BROADHEAD: Hallam's already had the other three.

CROOKES: He had three for buying a pistol with - what we never used. I used my own gun - my air-gun.

BROADHEAD: I don't see that's any of my business, Sam.

CROOKES: It could be your business if anything happened to him.

BROADHEAD: Who?

CROOKES: Linley. He's - he's hurt bad.

BROADHEAD: How bad?

CROOKES: I don't know. Bad enough. I got him in t' head.

BROADHEAD: Whereabouts in the head?

CROOKES: Here. Just on his temple. I - I didn't aim at his head, I swear I didn't. But he moved. I aimed at his shoulder - to maim him, like, stop him working - like you said, but he moved.

BROADHEAD: I see. But he's not died yet, has he?

CROOKES: Not yet, no. I hope to God he doesn't.

BROADHEAD: Well, we'll have to wait and see, won't we? Is there owt else?

CROOKES: Well, there's -

BROADHEAD: What?

CROOKES: There's the other three pound, isn't there?

BROADHEAD (shakes his head): You'd best take your twelve, Sam. It's all we can pay.

(CROOKES, about to say more, thinks better of it and takes up the money. He turns to go.)

Sam . . . I think you'd best not be seen round here for a bit - not for a bit anyway. Tell Hallam.

(CROOKES looks at him and goes out. BROADHEAD very deliberately enters the amount paid in a book. Then he puts on his jacket, settles his gold eyeglass, and crosses. The MAYOR and several CITZENS are waiting for him. Polite applause. The MAYOR rises.)

MAYOR: Gentlemen. It is my very willing duty today, and I may say my very great pleasure, to be called upon to publicly acknowledge the esteem in which we hold one of the better-known of our citizens.

CITIZENS: Hear, hear.

MAYOR: I have in my hand a very handsome address prepared by Mr Dronfield, and before presenting it to the worthy recipient, I would like to read it to you.

Sir, - We, the undersigned, having read in the columns of the *Sheffield and Rotherham Independent* newspaper your temperate, yet firm and unflinching defence of well-regulated trade unions, in answer to 'Sheffielder', 'Vulcan' and others, take this opportunity of expressing our sincere gratification to you in having so ably placed before the public the benefit of such unions, when properly conducted alike for the employers and the employed. With every sincere wish that you and yours may long live to enjoy the esteem and confidence so honourably and so fearlessly earned, we beg respectfully to subscribe our names.

And the address, gentlemen, is signed by some eleven Secretaries of Trade Unions in this town.

CITIZENS (applause): Good Owd Smeetem.

MAYOR: I should like to add, gentlemen, that the presentation of this address is alike honourable to the recipient and creditable to the trade.

CITIZENS: It is an' all.

(Cheers.)

MAYOR: It does not fall to the lot of many to receive from their fellow-townsmen such a united expression of esteem as characterizes this address. It shows, if I may quote:

Honour and shame from no condition rise;

Act well your part, therein the honour lies.

Mr Broadhead, I take great pleasure in handing you this document.

CITIZENS (applause): Speech, Speech!

(BROADHEAD takes the address from the MAYOR.)

BROADHEAD: Mr Mayor, Ladies and Gentlemen, Brothers. May I express my high appreciation of the honour you do me in presenting me with this handsome address. I am not a controversially-minded man by nature, but I must say that the, yes, the slanderous imputations which are all too often cast these days upon the trade unions do no less than to make my blood boil. So much so that I have felt bound to defend them to the best of my humble ability - which, I must say, my friends, have here much over-rated - By far - (Cries of 'No, no'.) - I have been a trade unionist, gentlemen, from my cradle, and I am probably looked upon by some as a very terrible character simply for that reason . . . (Polite laughter.) Well, I will not attempt at this time and in this assembly to defend my character, but I will go so far as to say this. I can assure you, Mr Mayor, ladies and gentlemen, and I say this publicly for the benefit of any who may be listening, that I would not do a dishonourable action, no, not even to save my life. (Applause.)

Street. Two WORKMEN of the Consumers' Gas Company enter with shovels.

FIRST WORKMAN: Here we are then.

SECOND WORKMAN: Aye, I'll just mark it out.

(The SECOND WORKMAN begins to pace out a rectangle on the ground for digging, making marks at the four corners with his heel.)

I think that'll be enough for a start.

FIRST WORKMAN: Oh, plenty.

SECOND WORKMAN: And don't forget what Mr Flintoff told us.

FIRST WORKMAN: What?

SECOND WORKMAN: About them other lot. If United Company's navvies turns up, he says, there's to be no unpleasantness like there was last time.

FIRST WORKMAN: I didn't start it, you know.

SECOND WORKMAN: It doesn't matter who started it. It was a very painful incident, Mr Flintoff said, and it's not to happen again.

FIRST WORKMAN: What do we do then, if they do turn up?

SECOND WORKMAN: We have to be polite to 'em.

FIRST WORKMAN: Eh?

SECOND WORKMAN: He said we have to be polite. We don't have to aggravate 'em. We just do our job and let them do theirs.

FIRST WORKMAN: Oh, I see.

(They start to dig.)

SECOND WORKMAN: Hey, they're here.

(Two United Company WORKMEN appear, with shovels.)

Now don't forget. Don't aggravate 'em . . . . Afternoon!

THIRD WORKMAN: Aye, aye!

(The FIRST and SECOND WORKMEN dig. The THIRD and FOURTH lean on their shovels with exaggerated unconcern. The FIRST WORK-MAN whistles a tune.)

Quite a good day for diggin'.

FIRST WORKMAN: Pardon?

THIRD WORKMAN: I say it's quite a good day for diggin'.

FIRST WORKMAN: Oh, aye, very nice.

(The THIRD and FOURTH take up a shovelful of the earth dug out by the FIRST and SECOND and carefully put it back again. The FIRST and SECOND pause, look at each other, then in unison dig out a shovelful each, placing it carefully on the side, then wait as the THIRD and FOURTH put it back. They continue this performance during the dialogue.)

FOURTH WORKMAN: Town's been very quiet lately.

SECOND WORKMAN: Very quiet, aye. Not much doin'.

FOURTH WORKMAN: Let's see, there hasn't been an 'orrible outrage for a couple of weeks now.

SECOND WORKMAN: They reckon they're going to put a stop to 'em, you know.

THIRD WORKMAN: Who?

SECOND WORKMAN: You what?

THIRD WORKMAN: Who is?

SECOND WORKMAN: Why, t' Queen and them. Government.

FIRST WORKMAN: Queen's not interested in us - I say . . .

THIRD WORKMAN: What?

FIRST WORKMAN: If you'd just hold your shovel ready, like, I could put muck straight on it. It'd save you bending.

THIRD WORKMAN: Oh, I will do, then. Happen I can do t' same for thee.

FIRST WORKMAN: Aye, thanks very much.

(They continue in this fashion, carefully placing the earth on each other's shovels.)

SECOND WORKMAN: It'll not be t' same, though.

FOURTH WORKMAN: What'll not?

SECOND WORKMAN: I mean, if they stop blowing each other up and that. It'll not be t' same. Newspaper'll not be worth gettin'.

FIRST WORKMAN: I don't see how they can.

THIRD WORKMAN: What?

FIRST WORKMAN: Stop 'em. They've had 'em as long as I can remember. Sheffield wouldn't be Sheffield without its shockin' 'orrible outrages.

THIRD WORKMAN: Some folk think about nowt only interfering with another man's pleasure . . . Hey, we're running' out o' muck.

FIRST WORKMAN: Hold on, I'll get another shovelful. (To SECOND WORKMAN.) And one for thee too; tha might as well earn tha wages.

SECOND WORKMAN: They reckon they will stop 'em. That's why they're havin' this inquest.

FOURTH WORKMAN: Why, who's dead?

SECOND WORKMAN: Nobody's dead. Some of t' masters want 'em to come from London to 'ave an Inquiry for looking into things 'ere in Sheffield.

THIRD WORKMAN: Oh. Well, if they do - I reckon they'll turn over a lot more muck than we have this afternoon. (Dirt from his shovel falls on FIRST WORKMAN.)

FIRST WORKMAN: Hey, watch it.

THIRD WORKMAN: What's up?

FIRST WORKMAN: Th'art supposed to be puttin' thy muck on my shovel, not on me, tha knows.

THIRD WORKMAN: Sorry . . . (Sneezes; dirt falls again on FIRST WORK-MAN.)

FIRST WORKMAN: Tha's done it again.

THIRD WORKMAN: Nay, I haven't.

FIRST WORKMAN: Tha has. Tha did it a purpose.

THIRD WORKMAN: It weren't a purpose.

FIRST WORKMAN (slinging a shovel-load of earth at him): Well, that were.

THIRD WORKMAN: Reet. If that's road tha wants it.

(He slings a shovelful back.)

SECOND WORKMAN (who has caught most of it): Hey, watch what th'art doin'.

(He slings earth at the THIRD WORKMAN which hits the FOURTH WORKMAN.)

The earth-battle sc

FOURTH WORKMAN: You mucky rotten devil.

(All four are now engaged in slinging earth at each other. The earth-battle quickly develops into a direct fight with spades. FLINTOFF enters in some alarm, and attempts to separate the two factions.)

FLINTOFF: Gentlemen, please - we shall have the entire town about our ears - the police - now please, lads, please have a little - remember the dignity of labour, gentlemen . . . Gentlemen, can I offer any of you a *drink.*

(At the word 'drink' the battle ceases as if the men had been turned to stone.)

FIRST WORKMAN: Who said drink?

FLINTOFF: There is, there must be, a beerhouse in the neighbourhood. You may - er - knock off for a few minutes. I'll see that your refreshment is paid for.

SECOND WORKMAN: They'll not serve you round here without you pay on t' nail, you know.

FLINTOFF: Oh . . . (Digs in his pocket.) . . . oh, well, in that case, perhaps I'd better . . . there you are.

(FLINTOFF gives money to the FIRST and SECOND WORKMEN who speak together.)

FIRST WORKMAN: Thank you, sir.

SECOND WORKMAN: Thank you, Mr Flintoff.

FIRST WORKMAN: - And your very good health . . . come on . . .

(The FIRST and SECOND WORKMEN go off. FLINTOFF turns and sees the THIRD and FOURTH WORKMEN waiting expectantly.)

FLINTOFF: Oh . . . yes, well I suppose I can stand you a drink without being suspected of bribing a rival's employees . . . there you are.

(The THIRD and FOURTH WORKMEN touch their caps and go off, passing IRONSIDE entering.)

IRONSIDE: Were those our men, Mr Flintoff?

FLINTOFF: Yes - er - no; that is, some were and some weren't . . . Mr Ironside, I'm afraid this business is beginning to get quite out of hand.

IRONSIDE: Nonsense, sir. Teething troubles, that's all they are - teething troubles. I've always remarked that philanthropic work of any kind is peculiarly prone to teething troubles. We shall win through, Mr Flintoff - and the unfortunate poor of Sheffield will bless our names.

(A door opens suddenly and a WOMAN emerges.)

WOMAN: What's all this muck on my doorstep?

IRONSIDE: I beg your pardon, madam?

WOMAN: I heard you, you know.

FLINTOFF: There must be some -

WOMAN: Lakin' about in t' muck and using language - at your age, and all. I heard you, don't think I didn't.

IRONSIDE: Do you seriously suggest that Mr Flintoff and I -

WOMAN: Well, you can just get it cleaned up again, t' pair on you. I've only hollystoned that step this mornin', and look at it . . .

IRONSIDE: But my good woman -

WOMAN: I'm not havin' any argy-bargy about it. Here!

(She thrusts a bass broom at FLINTOFF and reaches inside the door for a shovel, giving it to IRONSIDE.)

Now you can just get it swept up.

(She goes in and bangs the door.)

IRONSIDE: Well! . . . If that virago seriously imagines for one moment that I, a Town Councillor, and you, a Company Secretary, will . . . !

(IRONSIDE throws down the brush, marches to the door, and is about to knock. The door opens and the WOMAN's head emerges.)

WOMAN (before he can speak): And if it happens again you'll get a bucket of slops on you.

(She withdraws and slams the door.)

IRONSIDE: There! You see, Flintoff? There is no limit to the ungratefulness of the common people. You slave to bring them the benefits of modern progress, and what do you get? Vulgarity.

FLINTOFF: I begin to wonder if they really want gas.

IRONSIDE: Want it? Of course they don't want it. They don't want education, they don't want religion, they don't want the Mechanics' Institute, they don't want morality and decency; but by Joshua they shall have these things if I have to ram them down their throats. And by Joshua they shall have gas! - Take off your coat.

(IRONSIDE begins to remove his jacket.)

FLINTOFF: My coat?

IRONSIDE: Well you can't dig a trench in a frock-coat, can you?

FLINTOFF: I - well, I -

IRONSIDE: Come on, off with it.

(IRONSIDE picks up a shovel left by one of the men, and starts to dig energetically.)

FLINTOFF: Mr Ironside, isn't it about time we started to face facts?

IRONSIDE (diggin): Facts? What facts? The only facts I'm concerned with at the moment are that gas needs pipes and pipes need ditches. What are you waiting for?

FLINTOFF: We cannot continue much longer without Parliamentary sanction. - We're not legal, Mr Ironside.

(The WORKMEN appear, unnoticed by IRONSIDE and FLINTOFF, and watch solemnly.)

IRONSIDE: Don't bother me with that now.

(The THIRD and FOURTH begin quietly to replace the earth dug by IRONSIDE as he throws it out. He doesn't notice.)

FLINTOFF: The Old Company can frustrate everything we do.

IRONSIDE: The Old Company is a donkey - it needs to be wolloped; and it will be wolloped if I've anything to do with it.

FLINTOFF: I think it's we who are being wolloped, not them. If we dig trenches, they fill them in; if we lay pipes they sabotage them with tunnels from cellars, and blame us for the leakage of gas. We've caused more explosions recently than the trade union terrorists; we've had lawsuits, flooded ditches, hostility from the magistrates, and the roof of the retort house falling in.

IRONSIDE: Is that all?

FLINTOFF: No. We are also practically bankrupt.

IRONSIDE: Trivia, my dear sir; negligible trivia.

(The OLD MAN has entered, with a newspaper.)

FLINTOFF: But the law -

IRONSIDE: Don't talk to me about the law. Where would our great trade union movement be if it had waited for the law? Where will the Consumers Gas Company be if it waits for the law.

OLD MAN: Hey! There's a bit about them in today's paper.

IRONSIDE: What?

OLD MAN: Aye. It has it here - 'New Gas Company ordered to amalgamate!'

IRONSIDE: Ordered to what?

OLD MAN: Amalgamate - it means, like, merge, you know . . .

IRONSIDE: I know perfectly well what it means, man. Give me that paper.

(He snatches the newspaper.)

OLD MAN: Cost me a penny, that did, you know . . .

IRONSIDE (reading): 'A Parliamentary Committee today decided that the only satisfactory solution to the New Gas Company's difficulties would be the immediate cessation of its activities, and an early amalgamation with the existing United Gas Company.'

(He lowers the paper, folds it deliberately, and drops it in the trench.)

(Quietly.) Amalgamation . . . amalgamation, Mr Flintoff.

FLINTOFF (solemnly): Yes, Mr Ironside.

IRONSIDE: Your hand, please.

(FLINTOFF helps him out of the trench.)

My coat.

(FLINTOFF helps him into his coat.)

(Bursting out) Damn and blast their amalgam . . . ! (He controls himself with a great effort.) . . . Mr Flintoff, this is my last and final attempt to bring the benefits of progress to the people of Sheffield. They do not deserve it.

(A door opens. The WOMAN emerges.)

WOMAN: Can you smell gas?

IRONSIDE: No, madam. Gas is a subject in which I no longer have the slightest shadow of interest.

WOMAN: Well, it can't be drains, cos there is none.

IRONSIDE: That doesn't surprise me . . . no drains? Of any kind?

WOMAN: You don't think Council'll ever put proper drains in round here, do you?

IRONSIDE: Disgraceful. What kind of sanitary arrangements exist in your house?

WOMAN: You what?

IRONSIDE: Do you have a closet?

WOMAN: Aye, you can come through and use it if you're desperate.

IRONSIDE: I merely wish to know what kind it is.

WOMAN: We've a midden, same as everybody else.

IRONSIDE: That's what I thought . . . Mr Flintoff, there is a fundamental answer to the social and moral ills of this town - why couldn't I see it before - of course - sewerage, Mr Flintoff, sewerage! . . . Now I have a scheme in mind . . . Mr Flintoff . . . Mr Flintoff!

(But FLINTOFF has gone. SINGERS have entered and all join in 'Gas Company Song'.)

BROADHEAD discovered on park bench, reading a volume of Shakespeare. CROOKES enters and goes over to him.

CROOKES: You wanted to see me, Mr Broadhead?

BROADHEAD: Yes, Sam. You know, there's a great deal of truth to be found in the works of the Bard.

CROOKES: Who?

BROADHEAD: The Bard. William Shakespeare. 'There is a tide in the affairs of men' he says, 'Which taken at the flood, leads on to fortune'. That's what I've always done. Take it at the flood. Act when the time is ripe; he's right, you know.

CROOKES: Was it about John Helliwell?

BROADHEAD: What do you say, Sam?

CROOKES: I say was it about John Helliewll as you wanted to see me, because we've been after him, only we was mistook about where he works.

BROADHEAD: Leave him be.

CROOKES: What?

BROADHEAD: Leave him be. There's something more important cropped up, and I'd like you and Hallam to attend to it.

CROOKES: What's that, then?

BROADHEAD: Wheatman and Smith's. You know their works, do you?

CROOKES: I know where it is. Kelham Island, int it -

BROADHEAD: Yes. Well, Wheatman and Smith's have just had machinery put in.

CROOKES: What sort of machinery?

BROADHEAD: For grinding straight saws. There's over fifty skilled saw-grinders out of work this minute, living off the union box, and Wheatman and Smith's put in machines that'll mean turning more off. Well, the time to hit 'em is now, and hit 'em hard. (He opens a purse and takes out money.) Here's a couple of sovereigns.

CROOKES: What's that for?

BROADHEAD: You'll be wanting to buy a few pounds of gunpowder, I daresay. Well, buy plenty.

CROOKES: What shall we do, go for their chimney?

BROADHEAD: Up to you, Sam. I never interfere in the details. Just as long as Messrs Wheatman and Smith know we mean business, that's all.

CROOKES: It'll not be so easy, Mr Broadhead.

BROADHEAD: Justice never is easy. But that's what it is - justice - whether the law thinks so or not.

CROOKES: I mean, it'll not be an easy job getting in. What're we to have for it?

BROADHEAD: I daresay the funds can stretch as far as fifteen pound - if you'll take it in instalments. We're down on contributions with so many being laid off.

CROOKES: I'll tell Hallam tonight..

BROADHEAD: Aye, you see him. I'd rather deal with you than him.

CROOKES: Right. Is there owt else, is there?

BROADHEAD: No, I don't think so - only be careful. I wouldn't like to see you hoist with your own petard, as the poet puts it.

CROOKES: With me what?

BROADHEAD: With your own bottle of gunpowder.

CROOKES: I'll watch it. Goodnight, Mr Broadhead.

BROADHEAD: Goodnight, Sam.

(CROOKES goes out.)

(To himself.) 'And't shall go hard, but I will delve one yard below their mines, and blow them at the moon.'

The interior of a public house. A few customers quietly drinking. The OLD MAN enters, muffled up.

OLD MAN: By the frost, it's about as cheerful in here as it is outside. What's up, then - are you all i' mourning or summat?

FIRST WORKMAN: Aye, mourning for thee.

OLD MAN: Me? I'm nowhere near dead yet; not as I know of, any road.

FIRST WORKMAN: Then it's time somebody told thee.

(The OLD MAN puts money on the counter.)

BARMAN: Here, what's this?

OLD MAN: What's it look like? Tuppence for me pint.

BARMAN: It's tuppence ha'penny.

OLD MAN: Eh?

BARMAN: It's tuppence ha'penny in here. Tuppence int tap.

OLD MAN: Oh, I'm supping wi' t' nobs, am I? I'd never have guessed it. I'll toss thee for the odd ha'penny.

BARMAN: Tha will not. Hand it over.

OLD MAN (paying): Younger generation! You've neither sport no nowt in you -

(A young WOMAN enters with a BLIND BEGGAR and sings 'I'm a Collier Lass, and I'm come o'er from Barnsley'.)

WOMAN (sings): My name is Polly Parker, I' come o'er from Barnsley, My father and mother work in the coal mine,

Our family's large, we have got seven children,
So I am obliged to work in the same mine.
And as this is my fortune I know you feel sorry
That in such employment my days I shall pass,
But to keep up my spirits, I sing and look merry,
Although I am only a poor collier lass.

By the greatest of dangers each day I'm surrounded,
I hang in the air by a rope or a chain,
The mine may fall in, I may be killed or wounded,
May perish by damp or the fire of a train,
But though we go ragged and black are our faces,
As kind and as free as the best we'll be found,
And our hearts are as white as your lords in fine places,
Although we're poor colliers that work underground.

I am now growing up fast somehow or other.
There's a collier lad strangely runs into my mind
And in spite of the talking of father and mother,
I think I should marry if he was inclined.
But should he prove surly and will not befriend me,
Another and better chance may come to pass,
And my friends here I know, to him will recommend me,
And I'll be no longer a poor collier lass.

SECOND WORKMAN: Now I'll give you one.

OLD MAN: Why, what have we done to thee?

FIRST WORKMAN: Get on tha can't sing thee.

SECOND WORKMAN: I can do owt when I've had a few.

FIRST WORKMAN: Thee? Tha can't even sing 'God Save the Queen'.

SECOND WORKMAN: Who can't? (Sings.) - 'God Save our Gracious . . .'
(He is sick.)

OLD MAN: It's a judgement on thee.

FIRST WORKMAN (bawling): God save great Thomas Payne
His Rights of Man to explain -

(The rest laugh and join in.)

To ev'ry soul.
He makes the blind to see
What dupes and slaves they be
And points out liberty
From pole to pole.

Thousands cry, 'Church and King',
That well deserve to swing
All must allow.
Birmingham blush for shame
Manchester do the same

The workman's recitation in the pu

Infamous is your name
Patriots vow.

(Two WORKMEN do a clog dance to the following verse.)

Why should despotic pride
Usurp on ev'ry side
Let us be free:
Grant Freedom's arms success
And all her efforts bless
Plant through the universe
Liberty's tree.

(Cheers; some deprecatory comments, and general comments.)

SECOND WORKMAN (standing up): It's the wonder of wonders this mighty steam hammer.

FIRST WORKMAN: Eh? What are tha talking about?

SECOND WORKMAN: Shut up, it's a recitation.

FIRST WORKMAN: Recitation! Recitation!

SECOND WORKMAN: It's the wonder of wonders this mighty steam hammer
What folks say it will do, it would make anyone stammer;
They say it will cut files as fast as three men and a lad,
But two out of three, it's a fact they are bad.

FIRST WORKMAN: They are an all.

OLD MAN: Down with machines!

FIRST WORKMAN: Shut thy gob, he's not finished.

SECOND WORKMAN: They say it will strike three hundred strokes in a minute,
If this is a fact, there will be something serious in it;
The tooth that is on them it looks fine to the eye,
But they're not worth a rush when fairly they're tried.

These Manchester cotton lords seem mighty keen
To take trade from Old Sheffield with this cutting machine;
They've a secret to learn - they know it's a truth -
The machine's naught like flesh and blood to raise up the tooth.

So unite well together by good moral means,
Don't be intimidated by these infernal machines;
Let them boast as they will - and though the press clamour,
After all, lads, there's naught like wrist, chisel and hammer!

(Cheers and applause.)

OLD MAN: Hey, I remember yo two now.

FIRST WORKMAN: Aye, I remember thee an all.

OLD MAN: It were yo wot dug that trench in front of our house, and then them other lot come and -

FIRST WORKMAN: Aw reet, aw reet, tha doesn't need tell everybody.

OLD MAN: How's the 'ole-digging trade, eh?

FIRST WORKMAN: I don't know. I packed it in.

OLD MAN: Never! Didn't they pay well, then?

FIRST WORKMAN: They paid all reet, but if every time tha digs a hole tha gets clobbered, there's not much future in it, is there?

OLD MAN: Who's winnin', then?

FIRST WOMAN: Who's winning what?

OLD MAN: Tha knows - United or Consumers. Who's winning?

FIRST WORKMAN: Don't ask me. They can all go and blow each other up for all I care.

(Muffled explosion off, rattling the room. Everyone keeps very still.)

Well, I'll go to bloody hell. They must have heard me.

GIRL: What were it?

BARMAN: Must be another gas-main gone up.

FIRST WORKMAN: Nay, they'll never be workin' at this time, and in this frost. It's summat bigger nor a gas main.

OLD MAN: It come from over yonder - t' other side o' t' river.

(An excited APPRENTICE and GIRL burst in.)

APPRENTICE: Did you hear it, did you?

WORKMAN: What were it?

APPRENTICE: Wheatman and Smith's - it's blowed up!

WORKMAN: Wheatman and Smith!

OLD MAN: Blowed up!

GIRL: Aye. A rare old thump it were, an' all. You should have seen t' chimney come down - like a pack o' cards.

FIRST WORKMAN: Come on, then. There might be somebody hurt.

(They all hurry out, chattering, leaving the place empty. Presently, when their noise has died away, HALLAM enters and goes to the bar. He knocks on the bar, waits and knocks again.)

HALLAM: Shop!

(No response. HALLAM shrugs, picks up the SECOND WORKMAN's glass and drinks it off. He looks at his hands, which are black, stuffs them in his pockets and goes out. The others return in ones and twos.)

GIRL: What's a few bricks and mortar when it belongs to t' masters.

OLD MAN (as he enters): Thee and thy pack o' cards! - Chimney's as good as ever it were.

GIRL: Well, it looked like it at first. I thought it were comin' down.

FIRST WORKMAN: You'd have thought a thump like that'd have done more damage, though.

SECOND WORKMAN: Aye, nowt only a few windows broke as far as I could see. (Reaches for his glass.) Hey! Who's supped my ale?

OLD MAN: Eh?

SECOND WORKMAN: There were t' best part of a pint here. Who's had it?

OLD MAN: Happen it were him as blew t' chimney down, eh? Ha, ha . . . I say happen it were him as - oh, well, ne'er mind . . .

VOICE (off): Think I'd better see whose in t' snug.

OTHER WORKMAN (enters): Hey, did you see all them coppers?

OLD MAN: What coppers?

OTHER WORKMAN: They must be some o' them extras what they fetched in for t' strike - about two dozen of 'em - all going like this -

(He imitates trotting policemen, truncheons ready. One or two others laugh and join in.)

Hey, I asked one of 'em what time it were, and all two dozen of 'em halted and pulled their watches out!

OLD MAN: Get off, th'rt a bigger liar than Soft Mick.

(All the WORKMEN are now parading as POLICEMEN.)

OTHER WORKMAN: It's reet. And I says, 'hey', I says, 'what are yo lot doing out at this time o' neet?' And one says, 'We've been sent to keep strikers down.'

MEN (singing): We've been sent to Sheffield town
Sent to keep the strikers down,
We've been sent -

OTHER WORKMAN: I says, 'What, of a Monday?'

MEN (singing): To Sheffield Town.

OTHER WORKMAN: I says, 'Nobody in Sheffield works on a Monday anyroad - we're all in t' boozer!'

OLD MAN: Tha can't half spin 'em.

MEN (singing): They made a fuss of us when we got there,
Met us with a band in Paradise Square,
We've been sent
To Sheffield Town.

We've got to guard the workshops day and night
Our Chief Constable says it's right.
We've been sent
To Sheffield Town.

Let the Sheffield workman do what he can
A constable can't be a union man
We've been sent
To Sheffield Town.

(WOMEN and CITIZENS sing the Thomas Payne song in opposition to
WORKMEN who parade as policemen.)

God save great Thomas Payne
His Rights of Man to explain
To ev'ry soul.
He makes the blind to see
What dupes and slaves they be
And points out liberty
From pole to pole.

Thousands cry, 'Church and King',
That well deserve to swing
All must allow.
Birmingham blush for shame
Manchester do the same
Infamous is your name
Patriots vow.

Why should despotic pride
Usurp on ev'ry side
Let us be free
Grant Freedom's arms success
And all her efforts bless
Plant through the universe
Liberty's tree.

(The POLICEMEN disperse the shouting and yelling crowd.)

ACT TWO

A Sheffield Street scene. The SINGERS are selling knives and singing.

SINGERS: Cum all yo cutlin heroes, wheresome 'er yo be,
    All yo wot works at flat-back knives, cum lissen unto me;
        A basketful for a shillin',
        To make 'em we are willin'
    For ahr flat-backs and spotted hefts we daily mun be sellin,
    Or swap 'em for red herrins, ahr bellies to be filling.

(FIRST WOMAN greets SECOND WOMAN passing with a baby in a shawl.)

FIRST WOMAN: Oh, hello, love.

SECOND WOMAN: Hello.

FIRST WOMAN: I see you've had it, then.

SECOND WOMAN: Aye. A little lad this time.

FIRST WOMAN: Another belly to fill, eh?

SECOND WOMAN: That's your way of looking at it. Me and Walter don't see it like that. He's welcome.

FIRST WOMAN: Oh aye . . . You're looking a bit peaky. Are you all right, are you?

SECOND WOMAN: We're managing.

FIRST WOMAN: I know what that means. Has Walter been laid off?

SECOND WOMAN: He's off sick with his chest.

FIRST WOMAN: Tck, tck . . . Chest, eh? . . . How old is he now?

SECOND WOMAN: He's three months.

FIRST WOMAN: No - Walter.

SECOND WOMAN: Oh, he'll be twenty five come Whit Tuesday. Why?

FIRST WOMAN: Oh, well, he'll be all right. He's a good five years' work in him yet at that rate.

SECOND WOMAN: What do you mean, five years?

FIRST WOMAN: That's what they reckon. Fork-grinders snuffs it at thirty, saw-grinders at thirty-eight, as a rule.

SECOND WOMAN: Cheerful, aren't you?

FIRST WOMAN: It's true as I'm stood here. I read it in t' paper t' other day. A drunken grinder lives longest because he doesn't work as long at his trade as a steady man does.

SECOND WOMAN: It's coming to summat if their only choice is between th' alehouse and t' cemetery, int it?

FIRST WOMAN: Well, that's what it said.

SECOND WOMAN: I don't believe it.

FIRST WOMAN: Mind you, they're only going on average. I shouldn't take it as gospel, or think as Walter's on his way out.

SECOND WOMAN: Thanks for t' ray of hope, I'm sure.

FIRST WOMAN: I believe in facing facts.

SECOND WOMAN: It's one thing facing 'em, it's another thing askin' 'em in for a cup o' tea. Is there any other titbits in what paper of yours as might cheer me up?

FIRST WOMAN: You know that feller died, don't you?

SECOND WOMAN: I thought there'd be summat. What feller?

FIRST WOMAN: That chap - Linley. He were shot at in Scotland Street. Don't you remember?

SECOND WOMAN: Oh, him . . . That's six month since.

FIRST WOMAN: Well, he's lingered ever since. Int it shockin'?

SECOND WOMAN: Aye. Poor thing.

FIRST WOMAN: Not as anybody like him, you know; but it's shockin' all t' same. Shockin'. And they haven't found out to this day who did it.

SECOND WOMAN: Poor thing.

FIRST WOMAN: But somebody knows, you know. You mark my words - somebody knows.

(NEWSBOY enters - 'Latest on Linley murder', etc. Several in street buy a paper. BROADHEAD gives his copy to CROOKES and HALLAM after glancing at it. He exits.)

CROOKES: 'The jury, after consulting a few minutes, returned a verdict of wilful murder by some person or persons unknown.'

HALLAM: Murder.

CROOKES: Aye, murder.

HALLAM: It weren't murder. It were accidental. Tha never meant to kill him. We none of us meant to kill him.

CROOKES: But we did kill him.

HALLAM: How can they call it murder when it weren't?

CROOKES: The law says it is. And if they find out, it's a hanging job.

HALLAM: I'll not say nowt to nobody. I swear to thee I'll not say nowt to nobody, Sam.

CROOKES: Tha doesn't need to do no swearin', because if they do find out, it'll be thee and him as well as me.

HALLAM: Eh?

CROOKES: Accessories. You're both accessories. So we don't need no oaths, because we're all in t' same boat. I think we'll trust one another; cos that's all we can do, int it?

HALLAM: I reckon so. I know one thing; it'll be some time afore I'm asking Owd Smeetem if he's any more odd jobs.

CROOKES: Tha doesn't know what tha'll do while thy belly drives thee to it.

(Singers enter with WILLIAM LENG, singing 'The City Toff'.)

SINGERS: Let me introduce a fellah,
       Lardy-dah! Lardy-dah!
A fellah who's a swell, ah!
       Lardy-dah!
Though limited his screw, yet
The week he struggles through it,
For he knows the way to do it,
       Lardy-dah! Lardy-dah!
Yes, he knows the way to do 'the Lardy-dah!

He wears a penny flower
       in his coat, Lardy-dah!
And a penny paper collar round his throat,
       Lardy-dah!
In his hand a penny stick,
In his mouth a penny pick,
And a penny in his pocket,
       Lardy-dah! Lardy-dah!
And a penny in his pocket, Lardy-dah!

(LENG tips SINGERS. All exit except LENG and MR TAYLOR, the OLD MAN of Act One.)

LENG: Ah, Mr Taylor?

OLD MAN: Aye, that's me. Josiah Taylor. Everybody knows Josiah Taylor. You from the insurance, are you?

LENG: No, I'm afraid not.

OLD MAN: Only she's expecting a bit of a pay-out, like, on her sister what passed on.

LENG: Oh. I'm sorry.

OLD MAN: It's all right. She were a funny woman. What can we do for thee?

LENG: Perhaps I'd better introduce myself. My name is Leng - William Leng. I'm the new editor of the *Sheffield Telegraph.*

Leng and Old Man Taylor

OLD MAN: Oh, aye, well we've considered taking it regular, but like I said to her, there's never that much in it to justify the expense.

LENG: I think you mistake my intention, Mr Taylor. I'm not trying to sell you the newspaper. I just wanted to talk to you, that's all.

OLD MAN: Oh. Oh, I see. Only anybody as comes asking after you these days, it's generally money as they're after.

LENG: Very true. No, I've only recently come to the town, you see, and there is much about it I have still to learn. So I have come to you, Mr Taylor. I'm told there are few things that have happened in recent years in Sheffield that you don't know about.

OLD MAN: Well, I've always kept me eyes and ears open, you know, and I've lived here a long time. Aye, I have that. What is it you want to know like?

LENG: Well, these so-called outrages. Can you tell me anything about those?

OLD MAN: Don't you read your own newspaper, then, Mr Leng?

LENG: A good point, Mr Taylor. Yes, of course we have a good deal of material in the *Telegraph* files, but I also like to talk to men like yourself who have lived through these times.

OLD MAN: I've lived through 'em all right, but I don't see what I can tell you that you don't know already.

LENG: One of the points that interests me is why these outrages have been allowed to go on so long.

OLD MAN: Ah, well, it's their living, you see.

LENG: Their living?

OLD MAN: Aye, of course it is. They're frightened men - frightened of their living - frightened of their lives, if it comes to that.

LENG: But it amounts to a reign of terror, Mr Taylor. Do none of these men dare speak out to protect them from threats and intimidations and from physical attack?

OLD MAN: If tha were a file-cutter, Mr Leng, with a wife and family near starvation more often than not, tha wouldn't need to ask a question like that. The law won't have nowt to do with trade unions, tha knows.

LENG (opening his notebook): But look at the record, Mr Taylor, over the past ten years. Elisha Parker, whose house was blown up, and who was shot; James Linley, who was shot at, attacked with gunpowder and eventually tracked down and killed; Samuel Baxter, blown up; Joseph Helliwell, blown up and blinded; Joseph Wilson, John Helliwell, George Wastnidge, Samuel Sutcliffe - all victims of personal attack - some forty or fifty cases of industrial outrages involving injury to the person -

OLD MAN: Tha doesn't need to tell me, I remember 'em all.

LENG: And out of all these men, not one has dared to stand up in court and name the perpetrators of these crimes?

OLD MAN: Not while trade unions is a bad smell to them as runs this country, they won't. Trade matters is trade matters, and they'll not talk.

LENG: Mr Taylor, have you ever heard the expression 'Owd Smeetem'?

OLD MAN: Owd Smeetem? Aye . . . I have heard it. Aye.

LENG: Can you tell me what it means?

OLD MAN: Well, it's like a nickname - you know? - it means, well, owd smite 'em - clobber 'em, owd hit-em-hard.

LENG: Old hit-them-hard. Do you know a man of that name, or nickname?

OLD MAN: Oh well, nobody in particular, you know, I mean . . . no, I can't say I know who they mean when they say Owd Smeetem. No, I don't. I'm sorry, no.

LENG: As you say, Mr Taylor . . . frightened men.

OLD MAN: Ah?

LENG: Well, you've been very courteous and patient, Mr Taylor - I appreciate it. (Taking out a sovereign.) Will you allow me to buy you a drink?

OLD MAN: That's very civil of you, I'm sure.

LENG: Good day, Mr Taylor.

OLD MAN: Good day to you, sir . . . Mr Leng!

LENG: Yes?

OLD MAN: There's a feller as wears a gold eyeglass. Big chap. He can hit hard sometimes.

LENG: Thank you, Mr Taylor.

(The OLD MAN nods and goes in.)

The 'Royal George'. LENG is waiting. BROADHEAD enters, putting on his coat.

BROADHEAD: You wished to see me, sir?

LENG: My name is Leng, Mr Broadhead. I am the new editor of the *Sheffield Telegraph.*

BROADHEAD: Indeed. A fine, outspoken paper, if I may say so.

LENG: Thank you. I don't wish to trouble you, especially after working hours, but I feel it incumbent upon me to make a point of meeting as many of the outstanding people of the town as I can . . . I'm not, er, taking up your time, I hope?

BROADHEAD: No, no. I have a few small matters of correspondence to attend to, but they can wait.

LENG: You are very kind. As secretary of a large union, you must be a very busy man, I'm sure.

BROADHEAD: Work that I am proud to do, Mr Leng. It is an honour, rather than a duty, to serve one's fellowmen in whatever capacity.

LENG: I am sure you are right. It is the saw-grinders' union, is it not?

BROADHEAD: Yes, sir, the saw-grinders; which includes the allied unions of the saw-makers and the saw-handle-makers. It is a position of some responsibility - and to me, as I say, one of honour.

LENG: 'Honour and shame . . . '

BROADHEAD: Hm?

LENG: Forgive me, I was quoting.

BROADHEAD: Ah.

LENG: 'Honour and shame from no condition rise . . . ' How does it go?

BROADHEAD: ' . . . Act well your part, therein the honour lies.'

LENG: Act well your part. Yes . . . Mr Broadhead, it must be a source of some concern to you that an organization such as yours should attract so much unfortunate publicity from time to time.

BROADHEAD: I don't quite follow you, sir. What unfortunate publicity?

LENG: I refer to those incidents of violence within the trade which seem to have -

BROADHEAD: Pardon me, sir. Very few of these incidents of violence have been proved to be connected with the trade.

LENG: Well, imputed to the trade, shall we say -

BROADHEAD: Ah. Imputed. That is a very different matter. It is the imputation which causes me concern. And which causes concern to every responsible citizen of this town. Have not the letters I have published in your journal testified to my concern? Have not I and the officials of my union been so concerned for our good name that we have offered rewards of up to fifty pounds to any man who will come forward with information as to the instigators of these acts of outrage? You may rest assured that *I* am *very* concerned, sir.

LENG: I am glad to hear it, Mr Broadhead. I take it, then, you would not be averse to an official investigation into these affairs, to clear the good name of the unions?

BROADHEAD: An official investigation? What sort of official investigation?

LENG: It is my intention to conduct a campaign, Mr Broadhead, through the columns of my newspaper, to influence Parliament to institute a full Court of Inquiry into these matters.

BROADHEAD: Indeed . . . Do you think you will succeed, Mr Leng?

LENG: I am very confident of it. I think the time has come when public opinion will be strong enough to compel the Government to do it.

BROADHEAD: I see . . .

LENG: You are not averse to the idea of such an Inquiry?

BROADHEAD: So far from being averse to it, I would welcome it. These acts of violence and outrage have brought shame and disgrace for too long to the fair name of Sheffield. I wish you every success, sir.

LENG: Thank you. Good night, Mr Broadhead.

BROADHEAD: Good night, sir.

(LENG goes out as CROOKES enters. BROADHEAD takes off his jacket, and opens his account book.)

CROOKES: Who were that as just went out?

BROADHEAD: Him? . . . Only a busybody, Sam . . . thinks he can walk into a town and turn it upside down in two minutes. He'll learn . . . he's nowt a pound, him. I'll not be a minute, Sam. (Continues working. CROOKES bumps into table.) Now then, Sam - you've been drinking.

CROOKES: I've had a few. Owt doing, is there?

BROADHEAD: Well, I'm a bit worried about Fearnehough. I've had representations about him. There's them as thinks he should have summat done at him to stop him working.

CROOKES: He's at Butcher's Wheel, int he?

BROADHEAD: Yes.

CROOKES: Well, we can't ratten him theer. There's no road into that place - it's like Wakefield Jail.

BROADHEAD: We'll have to think of summat else, then, shan't we?

CROOKES: Where does he live?

BROADHEAD: Just a minute. (Consults his book.) New Hereford Street, I think.

CROOKES: Has he any family?

BROADHEAD: Family? Yes, I think so. Wife, daughter - and a couple of lads, I think. Why?

CROOKES: Nowt only . . .

BROADHEAD: Only what?

CROOKES: I don't like doing summat when there's kids.

BROADHEAD: I don't see as there's any other road, except -

CROOKES: I'm not using a gun no more - not after Linley.

BROADHEAD: Up to you.

CROOKES: Aye, it's always up to me, int it? . . . I'll need a couple of pounds for t' gunpowder.

(BROADHEAD silently finds a sovereign and gives it to him. CROOKES turns to go out.)

BROADHEAD: Sam.

CROOKES: What?

BROADHEAD: We've right on our side, Sam. Always remember that. We've right on our side.

CROOKES: Have we?

(He goes out. BROADHEAD watches him go.)

BROADHEAD (takes up scroll): Honour and shame from no condition rise, Act well your part, therein the honour lies.

(He exits.)

Three a.m. in Hereford Street. A drunk is trying to find his way home.

DRUNK (singing): St Patrick was a gentleman . . .
He came of decent people . . .

(He peers at the surroundings.)

Hereford Street? What the hell am I doing in Hereford Street? I wouldn't be found dead in Elephant Street . . .

(He struggles to light a clay pipe.)

(Singing): St Patrick was a gentleman
He came of decent people . . .

Decent people be damned; he was bloody Irish, weren't he? -

Comin over here, takin bread out of were mouths -
(Singing.) He built a church in Dublin Town
And on it put a steeple . . .

Well what the bloody hell else would he put on it, eh?
I ask you . . . Hey!

(This last to CROOKES, who has entered with a can of gunpowder bound round with a lash-line, the whole rolled in a bit of sacking.)

Have you got a light, have you?

(CROOKES shakes him off, and looks round for the house.)

Hey, do you know where I live? Eh? Do you?

CROOKES: No, I don't.

DRUNK: Cos I'm buggered if I do . . .

(He staggers away from CROOKES, and collapses on the ground. CROOKES disappears round a corner.)

Elephant Street, this is . . . Elephant Street . . . (Giggles.) Dost know what one elephant said to t' other elephant? It said: I don't know about thee, but I'm anellovanellovanellovanellovanellovanellovanelephant . . . And there's no elephants in Ireland, because Saint Patrick didn't hold wi' vermin;

His father was a Hollaghan,
His sister was a Grady,
His mother was a Milligan
And his wife the widow Brady . . .

(CROOKES returns without the package.)

DRUNK: Hey, thee! Doest tha know what one elephant said to t' other elephant, eh?

CROOKES: Oh, go home and go to bed.

(CROOKES hurries out.)

DRUNK: I'm going home . . . I'm going . . . I'm going . . . I'm going, you don't need push me . . . I'm going . . . I'm going . . . I'm bloody gone!

(The DRUNK falls asleep and snores. Very loud explosion. Dust, breaking glass. Silence, then a scream, falling to a woman's cries. The lights fade, and sobbing continues until the lights go up again on the same set, with a WOMAN, the wife of FEARNEHOUGH, sitting on a chair in the street. Her clothes are torn under the shawl she wears, her face and arms smudged with soot and dirt. She is in a very distressed state, sobbing continuously. A NEIGHBOUR and the husband FEARNEHOUGH are in attendance. A POLICEMAN in attendance. The DRUNK has gone.)

FEARNEHOUGH: Now come on love, it's all over now; you'll have to pull yourself together, you know.

MRS FEARNEHOUGH (shaking and sobbing): I can't Tommy, I can't stop shiverin' . . . I can't . . . I can't get warm . . . I can't . . .

(LENG enters. The NEIGHBOUR holds MRS FEARNEHOUGH close and cradles her head like a child.)

NEIGHBOUR: Now you're not hurt, there's nobody been hurt, hush love, hush - you're all all right . . . you're all right . . .

LENG (approaching FEARNEHOUGH): Mr Fearnehough? Can you tell me

what exactly happened, Mr Fearnehough?

FEARNEHOUGH: Nay, I don't know. We were all i' bed, fast asleep, all on us.

LENG: How many of you were in the house?

FEARNEHOUGH: Well, there were me and me wife, and my two lads, and ahr little lass. Kids have been taken to one o' t' neighbours, for to be cleaned up . . . poor little devils, it's terrible for 'em it is, terrible . . . But them as done it'll not get away wi' it this time, I'll tell you . . . we've had enough . . . I'll see as they don't get away wi' it, it doesn't matter who they are.

LENG: Have you any idea who it was, Mr Fearnehough?

FEARNEHOUGH: Idea? I've more than any idea. I know bloody well. I know who's at back of it all right, don't you fret.

LENG: Who? . . . Who, Mr Fearnehough?

FEARNEHOUGH: I'll say what I have to say at the proper time. I'm naming no names to you, not yet I'm not.

LENG: Oh, come on man - this may be the chance to put an end to this business.

FEARNEHOUGH: What business?

LENG: The whole of this dreadful series of outrages. We're ready to fight the battle, Mr Fearnehough, but we must have the facts. Now tell me - you know who it was, but do you have proof?

FEARNEHOUGH: Aye, I have.

LENG: You have? What proof?

FEARNEHOUGH: Threatening letters. Letters as said they'd blow up my house.

LENG: Have you still got them?

FEARNEHOUGH: Aye, I think so. They're in desk in t' front, if that's still there.

LENG: Come, show them to me.

FEARNEHOUGH: Hold on, I'm feelin' a bit - it's shook me, you know, and I'm not a young man.

LENG: Forgive me, I'm being thoughtless. Let me help you.

FEARNEHOUGH: Nay, I'm all right.

(LENG, FEARNEHOUGH enter the house. His WIFE's distress has subsided into the occasional shudder.)

NEIGHBOUR: Are you feelin a bit better now, love?

MRS FEARNEHOUGH: I think so, but I'm that cold . . . I'm that cold.

NEIGHBOUR: Come on, we'll go into our house for a bit.

The neighbour comforting Mrs Fearnehough

MRS FEARNEHOUGH: Where's Tommy? What have they done with Tommy?

NEIGHBOUR: He's all right. You're all all right. Now come on.

(LENG and FEARNEHOUGH re-enter, LENG shaking the dust from a few sheets of paper.)

I'm taking her into our house Tom.

FEARNEHOUGH: All right, luv.

(The NEIGHBOUR helps MRS FEARNEHOUGH off.)

LENG: They are all here?

FEARNEHOUGH: Aye, they are.

LENG: Well now, let's see. (Ruffles through the letters.) You know who wrote them?

FEARNEHOUGH: He did - Owd Smeetem - Broadhead.

LENG: All of them?

FEARNEHOUGH: There's nobody else it could have been.

LENG: They don't appear to be in the same hand, though.

FEARNEHOUGH: He can write two or three different sorts of hand — I've seen him do it.

LENG: These signatures - 'Mary Ann' - 'Tantia Topee' - what do they mean?

FEARNEHOUGH: They mean him - every man in t' trade knows what they mean. You get a note from 'Mary Ann' and you know he's after you.

LENG (scanning the letters): Their general tone is threatening, it's true, but wait a minute - here's a reference to Linley; there - what's the word there?

FEARNEHOUGH: I'm sorry, I'm no scholar - I couldn't tell you.

LENG: You can't read?

FEARNEHOUGH: No, sir. I had no proper schooling to speak of.

LENG: But you said you could recognize different sorts of hand.

FEARNEHOUGH: So I can. I can see if two lots of writing's in different hands, whether or not I can read 'em.

LENG: I see . . . (Reading.) . . . it looks like 'Linley's lead pills'?

FEARNEHOUGH: That's it. It says about cat's foot, and getting a dose of Linley's lead pills.

LENG: Cat's foot?

FEARNEHOUGH: It means, next time - they'd do for me proper. And they have an all.

LENG: Yes, I'm afraid they have. However, you are all alive, which is more than can be said for Linley. But this is it, Mr Fearnehough - this is certainly it; the beginning of the end for Old Smite-em. (Looks at watch.) And I think we're in time for today's edition.

LENG is at one side of the stage, BROADHEAD the other. Each is writing and is lit while he speaks.

BROADHEAD (reading): To The Editor of the *Sheffield Telegraph.* Dear Sir, The foul deed in Hereford Street adds to the fearful catalogue of such things which are disgracing the fair name of this increasing and prosperous town. All will join with me in condemning this foolishly insane and wicked practice . . . (Continues writing.) I am subscribing five pounds for the discovery of the offender.

(Light fades on BROADHEAD; comes up on LENG.)

LENG (reading): The *Sheffield Telegraph, October 22nd, 1866* . . . Must the Hereford Street explosion be suffered to count as another evidence of the power of the terrorists, another conclusive proof of the impotence of the law, another victory achieved by that despotism of diablerie which has so long mocked at justice and trampled under-foot all received opinions of public and private right? (He pauses.) Not so. (Writes.) Not so. The history of this town is too deeply stained already for that. The brand of Cain is imprinted upon it. We who have been employed for some days in collecting evidence about the matter have no moral doubt that the well-heads of these atrocities are to be traced by following up through all their windings the things that flow from them, comma - (He writes.) · and we will pledge our reputation that if this work of tracing backwards is done by a Commissioner (Capital 'C' - he inserts this.) - the revelations will be such as will startle the whole nation. The way to get at the Hereford Street savagery will be to go back beyond it by taking evidence on the various outrages which preceded it - outrages enveloped in mystery at the time, but at this hour capable of being used as guiding links in one single, tangible, and curiously welded chain. Um.

(He exits.)

The 'Royal George'. CROOKES waits nervously, holding a copy of the *Sheffield Telegraph.* BROADHEAD enters.

BROADHEAD: Now then, Sam. You want to see me?

CROOKES: What's this Commission they're talking about?

BROADHEAD: Did anybody see you come in here, Sam?

CROOKES: I don't think so.

BROADHEAD: Only as things are it might be better if you weren't seen round here at all for the present.

CROOKES: So there is summat in it, is there?

BROADHEAD: Nothing for you to worry about, nor me either.

CROOKES: What can they do?

BROADHEAD: I tell you, nothing we need to worry about. They'll ask a lot of people a lot of questions, but if these people keep their trap shut and mind how much they tell 'em, it'll all pass over.

CROOKES: Aye, but will they? Will they keep their trap shut?

BROADHEAD: They will if they know what's good for 'em.

CROOKES: What about him?

BROADHEAD: Who?

CROOKES: Hallam. I'm not so sure about him.

BROADHEAD: I've never been so sure about him; it's you that's generally wanted him with you on these jobs.

CROOKES: It's only because I know there's nowt he wouldn't do, but I've never trusted him.

BROADHEAD: I'll have a talk with him.

(CROOKES nervously rustles the newspaper.)

Don't *worry*, Sam . . . He'll know what the position is when I've finished with him.

CROOKES: I'm not bothered about all the other things, it's only Linley. We should never have done that, Mr Broadhead. If anybody gets on to that . . .

BROADHEAD: They won't. I'll tell you what it's about, this Inquiry. It's about the trade - that's all, just the trade. There'll be a certain amount of muck turned over, I daresay. They'll find out about a few cases of rattening, and the odd clobbering in a back alley, but that's all.

CROOKES: You never know what they'll find once they start. One thing leads to another, and they're like bloody beagles, these lawyers, when they get a sniff of summat.

BROADHEAD: Lawyers? Is that what you're worried about? I might be only a working lad, and I might never have been to Oxford and Cambridge and that, but I'm a match for them. I'll make sure they get to know just as much as I want 'em to know. We're on our home ground here. We can blind 'em with science.

CROOKES: I hope you can, that's all.

BROADHEAD: I think you forget sometimes, Sam, I'm a big man in this town, and I'll be a big man when they've been and gone. Give me that paper.

(CROOKES gives him the newspaper.)

(Reading.) '. . . guiding links in a curiously welded chain . . .' I'll say one thing for our Mr Leng - he has a nice turn of phrase. But he'll find the chain's a bit too curiously welded for him to sort it out - or anybody like him. (Gives him letter.) 'Ere post that.

Street Scene: Full Company. The SINGERS move among the CROWD. Over the action we hear from time to time the SECRETARY to the Court of Inquiry as he reads about the Royal Proclamation.

SECRETARY: VICTORIA, by the Grace of God, of the United Kingdom of Great Britain and Ireland, Queen, Defender of the Faith.

TO Our right trusty and well-beloved Councillors.

WHEREAS it has been represented to Us that it is expedient that inquiry should be made into the several matters hereinafter mentioned.

NOW KNOW YE, that We, reposing great trust and confidence in your ability and discretion, have nominated, consituted, and appointed, and do by these Presents constitute, and appoint you to be Our Commissioners for the said inquiry.

AND WE do hereby enjoin you, or any Four of you, to inquire into and report on the Organization and Rules of Trades Unions and other Associations; with power to investigate any recent acts of intimidation, outrage or wrong alleged to have been promoted, encouraged or connived at by such Trades Unions or other Associations, and also to suggest any improvements to be made in the law with respect to the relations aforesaid, or with respect to the relations between Workmen and their Employers, for the mutual benefit of both parties.

Given at Our Court at St. James, the Twelfth day of February 1867, in the Thirtieth Year of Our Reign . . .

(NEWSBOY enters shouting, 'Buy your paper - Duke and Duchess of Norfolk visit Botanical Gardens - Great day for Sheffield - Royal visit to Botanical Gardens'.)

The Botanical Gardens on a warm summer evening. The PUBLIC are strolling about in their best, having been admitted as a great favour to admire the floral decorations for the Duke of Norfolk's visit. A BAND in the distance, playing waltzes. Among the strollers, two WOMEN.

FIRST WOMAN: Weren't them hydrangeas gorgeous?

SECOND WOMAN: I like a nice geranium myself.

FIRST WOMAN: It's cost a pretty penny on the quiet, that did.

SECOND WOMAN: I must say it's very good of 'em to open t' Botanical Gardens and let us have a look, though.

(A young GIRL joins them.)

GIRL: Oh, int it exciting? Did you see t' Duchess?

FIRST WOMAN: Mm. I was a bit disappointed in her hat. A bit more fruit would have helped it.

SECOND WOMAN: Aye. Fruit's dressy, I always think.

GIRL: I bet they had a good do, though - three hours they said it lasted.

FIRST WOMAN: What?

GIRL: Their dinner, like.

FIRST WOMAN: Wicked. How could anybody eat for three hours?

GIRL: Well, they did.

FIRST WOMAN: Wicked. No wonder there's all these Radicals.

SECOND WOMAN: Walter thinks there's going to be a revolution.

FIRST WOMAN: What does he know about it?

SECOND WOMAN: He's generally right, though. He said Prince Albert wouldn't live long, and he didn't.

FIRST WOMAN: Eh, look who's 'ere - in a crinoleen an' all.

SECOND WOMAN: It's that Mrs Brown.

(Enter MR and MRS BROWN.)

MRS BROWN: Oh, it's lovely up here. It reminds me of when we were kids and we used to have picnics at Brightside.

BROWN: You'd look well now with your picnic at side o' t' steam hammer.

MRS BROWN: We did, Dicky. It was all fields then, you know.

BROWN: Aye, fields and poachers . . .

MRS BROWN: Why not? You'd have gone short of many a rabbit pie if it hadn't been for one or two poachers I could mention.

OWN: Nag, nag, nag, you women have always got something to say.

(*The ballad* SINGERS, *who have been among the* CROWD *of sight-seers, come forward and sing 'The Jovial Cutlers'. The* STROLLERS *gather to listen, among them* LENG, *in earnest conversation with* JACKSON, *the Chief Constable.*)

SINGERS: Brother workmen, cease your labour,
Lay your files and hammers by;
Listen while a brother neighbour
Sings a cutler's destiny -
How upon a good Saint Monday
Sitting by the smithy fire,
Telling what's been done o' t' Sunday,
We in cheerful mirth conspire,
    Soon I hear the trap-door rise up,
    On the ladder stands my wife:
    'Damn thee, Jack, I'll dust thy eyes up.
    Thou leads a plaguy drunken life;
    Here thou sits instead of working,
    Wi' they pitcher on thy knee;
    Curse thee, thou'd be always lurking,
    And I may slave myself for thee.'

All you who, blinded by delusion,
Matrimony never know,
Cannot judge of my confusion,
But may think my tale untrue,
For her foul tongue it's past bearing,
Her looks are full of foul disdain;
Ranting, railing, tearing, swearing,
Hark! Her clapper rings again.
    'See thee, look what stays I've gotten,
    See thee, what a pair o' shoes;
    Gown and petticoat half rotten,
    Ne'er a whole stitch in my hose,
    Whilst broil'd up with noise and racket,
    Thou'd'st swallow more than would fill a butt -
    Damn it, tak' it - devil tak' it,
    It's better there than in thy gut.'

Now she speaks with motion quicker
Than my boring stick at a Friday pace;
She thows the generous sparkling liquor
With all her fury in my face;
My eyes, my apron, and my breeches,
My poor shirt sleeves are drench'd with ale.
Something bad my dear bewitches,

Again to vex us with her tale.
> 'Pray thee, look here, all the forenoon
> Thou's waste wi' thy idle way;
> When does t'a mean to get thy sours done?
> They master wants 'em in today;
> Thou knows I hate to broil and quarrel,
> But I've neither soap nor tea;
> Od burn thee, Jack, forsake thy barrel,
> Or never more thou'st lie wi' me.

Now once more on joys be thinking,
Since hard scolding's tired my wife;
The course is clear, let's have some drink in,
And toast a jovial cutler's life;
For her foul tongue, oh! Fie upon her,
Shall we our pleasures thus give o'er?
No! We will good Saint Monday honour,
When brawling wives shall be no more.

(The ballad over, the SINGERS move off and the STROLLERS move off, JACKSON leaves, and LENG comes forward to encounter BROADHEAD entering. He stops.)

LENG: Good evening, Mr Broadhead. A fine display in the gardens for the Duke of Norfolk, is it not?

BROADHEAD: Very fine, though I can't help thinking the money might not be better in the workers' pockets.

LENG: Spoken like a true Radical.

BROADHEAD: Well, your campaign has achieved its object, it seems.

LENG: Yes. I take it you will be attending the sessions of the Inquiry.

BROADHEAD: I shall.

LENG: As part of the Trades Unions Defence Committee, no doubt.

BROADHEAD: No, I am not a member of that committee.

LENG: You surprise me.

BROADHEAD: But as secretary of an important union, I consider it my duty to be there and to give what help I can.

LENG: Quite, quite. The Chief Constable tells me a great many depositions have been taken from a great many witnesses. The Inquiry will be a long one - some two or three weeks.

BROADHEAD: That is as it should be. It is important for the good name of the unions that the whole truth be told. Provided that it *is* the truth, Mr Leng.

LENG: Why should it not be?

BROADHEAD: These are illiterate men, sir, for the most part. Well-meaning,

Broadhead and strollers in the Botanical Gardens

but illiterate.

LENG: They still know truth from falsehood.

BROADHEAD: Maybe, but authority confuses them, and words are very easily put into their mouths - as a journalist you should know that.

LENG: What exactly are you trying to suggest, Mr Broadhead?

BROADHEAD: I think it would be a great pity if the ultimate good of the working men of this town were to be jeopardized for the sake of a few days of sensation in the columns of a newspaper.

LENG: If you think for one moment -

BROADHEAD: I think we should all examine our motives, Mr Leng. I am sure of mine; are you sure of yours?

LENG: Good day, Mr Broadhead.

BROADHEAD: Good day, Sir.

(LENG turns on his heel and leaves. CROOKES, who has been hanging about waiting for their talk to finish, draws BROADHEAD aside.)

CROOKES: Mr Broadhead!

BROADHEAD: What do you want? I told you to keep away.

CROOKES: He's done it.

BROADHEAD: What are you talking about?

CROOKES: Hallam, he's split.

BROADHEAD: What?

CROOKES: He's made a statement telling 'em everything.

BROADHEAD: Who? Telling who everything?

CROOKES: That newspaper feller for one.

BROADHEAD: Leng?

CROOKES: Yes, Leng. And Chief Constable Jackson. I told you. I told you he would.

BROADHEAD: Now just a minute. Are you absolutely sure about this?

CROOKES: He's told. He's made a statement and signed it.

BROADHEAD: Lots of men have been making statements - I told you: they'll find out a lot, I said they would, but most of it's trivial, it's rattening jobs and things like that. Everybody knows about them already. Now do you know for sure if he's told them about anything serious?

CROOKES: I don't know what he's told 'em, he's just told 'em, that's all, and t' little things lead to t' big things -

BROADHEAD: If you don't know what he's said to them, then we're no worse off. Now listen. A confession's only a confession - it doesn't *prove* anything. It can be made, and it can be denied. Now I shall be in that court every day, and when his turn comes, I'll be watching him. I'll see he denies it. He'll not own up to anything with me watching him. Now you get back to your work, and remember - don't come near me again, and if anybody asks you, you know nowt. Right?

CROOKES: Yes, Mr Broadhead.

BROADHEAD: Right, then.

(CROOKES goes out. Fade.)

The Council Hall in Norfolk Street, Sheffield. The Inquiry in session. BROADHEAD sits to one side, calm and unruffled.

CHAIRMAN: We are now in the seventh day of our hearing, ladies and gentlemen, and we have heard a great deal of testimony from a great many witnesses, but we still have a good way to go. I suggest we press forward with as little delay as possible.

But before we do, may I remind the Court of the following important point: The Act of Parliament which enables us to compel the attendance of witnesses, and to compel them to give answers to questions put to them, by the Court, also authorizes us to give to such witnesses a certificate of the fact; and, I must stress this, holding this certificate they cannot be proceeded against criminally, neither by the Government nor by a private person, for any act which they may have committed, provided that they make a full and fair disclosure of all the facts within their knowledge. The certificate we will give provides complete and absolute indemnity in law.

(To JACKSON.) Put up the next witness.

(Light on HALLAM, in the witness-stand.)

JACKSON: Hallam, Sir.

CHAIRMAN: Now, you are James Hallam?

HALLAM: Yes.

CHAIRMAN: Were you brought up as a saw-grinder?

HALLAM: Yes.

CHAIRMAN: When did you join the union?

HALLAM: When I was twenty-one years of age.

CHAIRMAN: How old are you now?

HALLAM: Twenty-nine years of age.

CHAIRMAN: Do you know of a firm called Wheatman and Smith?

HALLAM: Yes.

> (He looks at BROADHEAD, who settles his eyeglass firmly and watches him.)

CHAIRMAN: Had Wheatman and Smith a kind of machine that interfered with the trade?

HALLAM (in an undertone, avoiding BROADHEAD's stare): Not that I know of.

CHAIRMAN: Speak out.

HALLAM: Not that I know of.

CHAIRMAN: Did you ever try to blow up Wheatman's premises?

HALLAM (after a pause and a look at BROADHEAD): No.

CHAIRMAN: Were you ever solicited to blow them up?

HALLAM: No.

CHAIRMAN: Were you ever paid fifteen pounds to do business at Wheatman's to blow them up?

HALLAM: No.

CHAIRMAN: Did you ever try to put powder at the bottom of the chimney at Wheatman's.

HALLAM: No.

> (Pause.)

CHAIRMAN: I suppose you are aware that if you commit perjury, besides the penalty for that offence, you can be punished for what you have done?

HALLAM: I am perfectly aware of that.

CHAIRMAN: Have you never said that you were hired or engaged to blow up Wheatman's?

HALLAM: No.

CHAIRMAN: You never said that you bought gunpowder at Tibwell's of Snig Hill?

HALLAM: No.

CHAIRMAN: You never said that you went to the bottom of the engine-house chimney at Wheatman's, and that it was so hot that you could not put it in?

HALLAM: No. I never said nothing about it.

CHAIRMAN: Did you not say that you then put a quantity of gunpowder with a fuse up the drain, and went to Rutland Bridge and saw it explode?

HALLAM: No.

CHAIRMAN: And that on the following Saturday you went to Broadhead and he gave you fifteen pounds?

HALLAM: No.

(Pause.)

CHAIRMAN: Is it from fear of being personally injured that you do not speak out now, is that what you are afraid of? Are you afraid to tell the truth?

HALLAM: I would rather go on as we are doing.

CHAIRMAN: Is it fear of the consequences, not lawsuits, but fear of personal violence that prevents you telling more about it? Is that it?

HALLAM: I cannot answer that question.

CHAIRMAN: Is it fear of personal violence that prevents you telling us about it?

HALLAM: I cannot answer that question.

CHAIRMAN: But you must answer that question.

HALLAM: I cannot answer it.

CHAIRMAN: If you do not, I will send you to prison.

HALLAM: I would rather go there than tell you.

CHAIRMAN: Why would you rather go there than tell me?

HALLAM: I do not like implicating another man.

CHAIRMAN: Um. I should have thought you would have had very little scruple about that; tell me the name of that other man?

HALLAM: I cannot.

CHAIRMAN: If you do not, I will send you to prison; if you do not tell me the name of that other man, you shall forthwith go to prison.

HALLAM: I will not tell you.

CHAIRMAN: You will not?

HALLAM: No.

CHAIRMAN: You know his name but you will not implicate him?

HALLAM: Yes.

CHAIRMAN: Although you know the name of the man, you refuse to tell us his name?

HALLAM: Yes.

(Pasue.)

CHAIRMAN: Now again I say to you that you are screened from all consequences if you tell me. Tell the truth and do not let me be driven into sending you to prison. Think of your position, and before any steps are taken. There is one chance more, and one only; what was the name of that man?

HALLAM: I cannot tell you.

CHAIRMAN: James Hallam, it is my duty to send you to the Wakefield House of Correction, for contempt of court, for refusing to answer a question that you are bound by law to answer. You will go there, and be kept there, for the period of six weeks from this time. Remove the prisoner.

(HALLAM, about to speak, catches the eye of BROADHEAD, thinks better of it, and goes out.)

A cell of the town police-station. HALLAM and JACKSON, the Chief Constable.

HALLAM: How long will it be before you send me to Wakefield? How long? He'll get away with it, don't you fret - like he allus does.

JACKSON: Why didn't you speak out yesterday morning, Jem?

HALLAM: I don't know.

JACKSON: You made me look a bit silly, you know. All that statement I took down off you, and you wouldn't own up to it. You could have got it all off your chest and finished. What got into you?

HALLAM: I don't know.

JACKSON: Was it him?

HALLAM: Happen.

JACKSON: He's only a man, you know. He's not God.

HALLAM: It's road he looks at you. I went in - I'd every intention - and then I saw him sitting there, polishing his bloody eyeglass. They'll not send him to Wakefield Jail, will they? Oh no, not him! He'll kill me - he'll kill me if I tell any more.

JACKSON: There's no telling what'll happen until this Inquiry's over. Listen Jem, you know about your certificate don't you?

HALLAM: Aye, I know.

JACKSON: You tell 'em everything - everything you know, and you get a certificate that puts you in the clear. With that certificate in your pocket, we can't prosecute you for anything - not even Linley.

HALLAM: I know.

JACKSON: But as things are, they can't give you that certificate - not till you tell 'em everything. And without it, you're a dead man, cos we'll have you now - we'll have you for Linley, and you'll hang. You'll hang, Jemmy, make no mistake about that.

HALLAM: Oh, God, I wish I'd never seen him, I wish I'd never . . .

(He breaks down.)

JACKSON: So if I was you, I'd go back into that court -

HALLAM: I can't. I can't go back in there, with 'em all looking at me; and him, looking at me . . .

JACKSON: You've got to, Jem, you've got to go back, and you've got to tell 'em.

HALLAM: I can't do it.

JACKSON: You must do it.

HALLAM: I can't face him and - and denounce him, I - I can't.

JACKSON: Listen, if we stood between you and him, could you do it then?

HALLAM: Eh?

JACKSON: If you couldn't see him, could you say it then?

HALLAM: I don't know.

JACKSON: If you couldn't see him; if you couldn't see his eyes?

HALLAM: Aye, it's his eyes . . .

JACKSON: I think you could. I think you'll have to, because they want you back.

HALLAM: What?

JACKSON: They want you back in court.

HALLAM: Oh, God!

JACKSON: And this time you'll tell 'em everything. Everything, mind. Now come on, they're waiting.

The courtroom. The court assembled. BROADHEAD is present. HALLAM is on the witness-stand. JACKSON is near him. HALLAM is under great nervous stress.

CHAIRMAN: James Hallam, the last time you were here you refused to tell us who was the person who was with you on a certain occasion. You have come here again today. Are you now prepared to tell us who that person is?

OLD MAN: He's too frightened.

(Noise in Court: CHAIRMAN raps gavel on table. HALLAM licks his lips, looks at BROADHEAD, and looks away. JACKSON moves to stand between him and BROADHEAD.)

CHAIRMAN: Are you now prepared to tell us who that person is?

HALLAM: Yes.

CHAIRMAN: Who was that person?

HALLAM: Samuel Crookes.

(Noise in Court from SPECTATORS.)

CHAIRMAN: When you were here before, I spoke to you about Wheatman's. Were you ever at Wheatman's?

HALLAM: Yes.

CHAIRMAN: Did any person speak to you about going before you went?

HALLAM: Yes, Crookes.

CHAIRMAN: What did he say to you?

HALLAM: He said we had a job to do there, to blow it up.

CHAIRMAN: Did you buy powder, and a bottle, and a fuse?

HALLAM: Yes.

CHAIRMAN: Then what did you do?

HALLAM: We went on Monday night to Wheatman's.

CHAIRMAN: When you got there, what did you do?

HALLAM: We put the bottle in the sough, in the drain.

CHAIRMAN: When you put the bottle in the sough, what did you do with it?

HALLAM: I lit the fuse.

CHAIRMAN: Did it make a great explosion?

HALLAM: Yes.

CHAIRMAN: Were there men in the building at work when you let this off?

HALLAM: Yes.

CHAIRMAN: Did you see Broadhead after that?

HALLAM: Yes. The day but one after.

CHAIRMAN: What did he say?

HALLAM: He said we had done very well.

CHAIRMAN: Do you know why Wheatman and Smith were blown up?

HALLAM: For putting a new machine in.

(Pause. HALLAM wipes his face and loosens his collar.)

CHAIRMAN: Now. Do you recollect the time when Linley was shot?

HALLAM (after a pause, very quietly): Yes.

CHAIRMAN: On the Saturday before, were you not seen in West Bar with a pistol in your pocket?

(HALLAM is silent.)

Say yes or no.

HALLAM: Yes.

CHAIRMAN: Where did you get that pistol from?

HALLAM: I bought it.

CHAIRMAN: For what purpose did you buy the pistol?

HALLAM (very distressed and almost inaudible): I - I . . .

CHAIRMAN: I ask you for what purpose did you buy that pistol?

(HALLAM shakes uncontrollably.)

Answer the question.

(HALLAM is unable to reply.)

For what purpose did you buy the pistol?

(HALLAM stares at him, rises shakily, and goes to the CHAIRMAN's table, holding it for support.)

HALLAM (hardly audible): I will tell the truth if I may have my certificate.

CHAIRMAN: You shall have your certificate; and if the man you implicate will come forward and make a clear statement, he too shall have his indemnity.

(HALLAM turns to go back to his seat, and sways, about to faint.)

CHAIRMAN: Look to him.

(HALLAM stumbles, half-fainting. The Chief Constable, JACKSON, catches him, half-carrying him back to the witness's chair.)

Is he all right?

JACKSON: I think so, sir. It's no more than a faint.

CHAIRMAN: He is not shamming?

JACKSON (slapping HALLAM's face lightly to bring him round): No, he's not shamming. It's genuine, he's coming round.

(HALLAM groans, and pushes JACKSON away.)

CHAIRMAN: Are you able to continue now?

HALLAM: Yes, I - I'm all right.

CHAIRMAN: You are sure? I do not wish to press you unless you are able.

HALLAM: Yes.

CHAIRMAN: Perhaps we had better move the witness a little closer. The witness's voice is rather faint.

(JACKSON helps HALLAM to his feet, moves the chair nearer the CHAIRMAN's table, and helps HALLAM to sit.)

Thank you. We shall continue, but you must tell me if you are in great distress. Now. You say that you bought a pistol; for what purpose did you buy it?

HALLAM: To shoot Linley.

CHAIRMAN: Was there anybody associated with you in shooting Linley?

HALLAM: Yes, Crookes.

CHAIRMAN: Who shot him?

HALLAM (choking over the words and twisting his hands together): I compelled Crookes to shoot him. I asked Broadhead one day what he was doing with Linley, and he told me he would have conversation with me on the following day. He asked me then what I could do with him, and I told him as I would make him as he wouldn't work any more.

CHAIRMAN: What did he say to that?

HALLAM: He asked me what I should want for doing it; I asked him if twenty pounds would be too much - he told me that he couldn't give above fifteen for it.

CHAIRMAN: Then what did you do?

HALLAM: We followed him - Linley - from one place to another; we found there was no chance with a revolver, so Crookes got the air-gun. We followed him for five or six weeks, perhaps more, nearly every night but Sunday night. We followed him.

CHAIRMAN: How was it at last? Where was he shot?

HALLAM: Scotland Street - they call it 'The Crown', I think - he was in the back room, in the snug. He was sitting with his left hand to the window. We saw him through the window. I told Crookes he was there.

CHAIRMAN: What did Crookes do?

HALLAM: He refused to shoot. He said - he said there was too many people about. So I said . . .

CHAIRMAN: What did you say?

HALLAM: I told him he was either to do it or I would do him.

CHAIRMAN: When you had told him that, what did he do?

HALLAM: He said there was no chance. I said I would do it myself and risk it. He told me -

CHAIRMAN: What did he tell you?

HALLAM: He said I mustn't attempt - I'd miss him - and that he'd risk it.

CHAIRMAN: And then?

(Pause.)

What did he do?

HALLAM: He shot him . . . We run away . . . through the alley into Peacroft.

CHAIRMAN: What did you get for shooting Linley?

Hallam receiving his certificate in court

HALLAM: Seven pound ten.

CHAIRMAN: Who gave you the money?

HALLAM: Broadhead.

(Consternation in Court.)

CHAIRMAN: Had you any quarrel with Linley?

HALLAM: No.

CHAIRMAN: Had you ever spoken to him in your life?

HALLAM: No, I never did so.

CHAIRMAN: What was your reason for shooting Linley?

HALLAM: For being obnoxious to the trade.

CHAIRMAN: I believe you are pretty generally in work, are you not?

HALLAM: Yes, I am in a very good situation, or I was before I came here.

CHAIRMAN: I do not know that you are worse off now; you have removed a load from your breast and that must have borne you down. But it is not for me to comment upon that. You may go.

(HALLAM looks uncertainly about.)

You are free to go.

(HALLAM looks at BROADHEAD; the latter, who has slumped down in his seat, raises his head slowly and looks, grey-faced, at HALLAM, attempt to rally himself and to put on his eye-glass, but it falls from his fingers. HALLAM looks away and goes out.)

CHAIRMAN: Mr Broadhead, it will be our duty to inquire fully into all that you have said and done in connection with these matters - you must be in attendance to give us information, when that information shall be required.

BROADHEAD (trying to pull himself together to answer): Will it . . . will it be necessary for me to attend every day?

CHAIRMAN: I cannot think it will be pleasant for you after this to attend in a Court of this kind, but you must be where you can be found.

BROADHEAD: I am ruined, but I cannot complain. I must bear it.

(BROADHEAD goes out.)

SINGER: I'm ruined, I'm ruined, but I can't complain;
My ruin, my ruin, has not been in vain.
For me diamonds and pearls
      And me place in Park Lane,
      I'd be ru-ru-ruined all over again.

terior of a Music-Hall on a Saturday night. The house is well patronized,
cluding a number of local celebrities such as Chief Constable JACKSON.
ie CHAIRMAN makes himself heard above the hubbub.

HAIRMAN: Thank you, ladies and gentlemen, for your kind appreciation.
  As an encore, and to satisfy those many among you who are obviously
  anxious to display their virtuosity in vocalization -

(Cheers and catcalls.)

that is, who think they can sing -

(Cheers.)

You are requested to join the incomparable Miss de la Fleur in her
celebrated rendering of 'She's Only a Bird in a Gilded Cage'.

(The GIRL SINGER leads the audience in singing 'She's Only a Bird in
a Gilded Cage'.)

NGER: The ballroom was filled with fashion's throng,
  It shone with a thousand lights,
  And there was a woman who passed along,
  The fairest of all the sights.
  A girl to her lover then softly sighed,
  'There's riches at her command',
  'But she married for wealth, not for love,' he cried,
  'Though she lives in a mansion grand.'

(Chorus.) She's only a bird in a gilded cage,
  A beautiful sight to see,
  You may think that she's happy and free from care
  She's not, though she seems to be.
  'Tis sad when you think of her waste life
  For youth cannot mate with age
  And her beauty was sold for an old man's gold,
  She's a bird in a gilded cage.

I stood in the churchyard just at eve
When the sunset adorned the west,
And I looked at the people who'd come to grieve
For loved ones now laid at rest.
A tall marble monument marked the grave
Of the one who'd been fashion's queen,
And I thought she'd be happier here at rest
Than to have people say when seen -

(Chorus.) She's only a bird in a gilded cage . . . (etc.)

(The number finished, the audience laugh and applaud.)

CHAIRMAN: Thank you, ladies and gentlemen, thank you. I hasten to assure you that you will again be seeing and hearing the incomparable Miss Blanche de la Fleur -

OLD MAN: Get off with you, she's Minnie Murgatroyd fro' Barnsley.

GIRL SINGER: Shut thee face, fatarse.

(Hoots and cheers. GIRL SINGER exits.)

CHAIRMAN: Nevertheless, my dear sir -

OLD MAN: Never-the-what?

CHAIRMAN: Nevertheless; our talented and captivating chanteuse will be appearing again for your further delectation in a very few moments. But now - (Coughs.) - excuse me, a little dryness of the throat - forgive me . . . (Coughs.) . . . but now -

OLD MAN: Have one with me, matey.

CHAIRMAN: Thank you, sir, thank you; may your whippets win and your rabbits live for ever, and if you haven't got a mother-in-law, have mine. (Drinks. Applause.) But now, ladies and gentlemen, if I may have your kind indulgence and attention for just a few moments, I should like to welcome to our little temple of Bacchus and Terpsichore . . .

FIRST WORKMAN: You mucky-minded devil.

CHAIRMAN: Bacchus and Terpsichore, sir.

FIRST WORKMAN: Tups what?

CHAIRMAN: Terpsichore.

FIRST WORKMAN: I've never 'eard it called that before.

CHAIRMAN: She was one of the nine Muses of Parnassus.

FIRST WORKMAN: I thought it was summat rude.

CHAIRMAN: Honi soit qui mal y pense, my good sir.

POTMAN (offering pint): Compliments of Mr Harbottle, sir.

CHAIRMAN: Thank you, Mr Harbottle, whoever you may be, but I must decline your generous offer.

OLD MAN: Sup it up.

FIRST WORKMAN: Knock it back.

CHAIRMAN: On the principle, ladies and gentlemen -

OLD MAN: Sup it.

ALL: Get it supped, etc.

CHAIRMAN: On the principle that circumlocutory utterances such as mine can only suffer from excessive lubrication of the oesophagus -

FIRST WORKMAN: Aye, we had one but cat ate it.

ALL (jeering): Cum on, get it down thee.

CHAIRMAN: Or in other words, enough's enough - basta! basta!

FIRST WORKMAN: What are you calling me - I'll be up there and thump
   thee in a minute.

OLD MAN: Sup it.

ALL (clapping in chorus): Sup it, sup it, get it supped.

CHAIRMAN: All right, all right - to avoid further altercation - your good
   health, Mr Harbottom.

FIRST WORKMAN: And yours, Cherrybottom.

   (CHAIRMAN drinks.)

MEN: Your flower's wilting, luv.
   Tha'll do thyself a mischief.
   Summat's coming loose.

CHAIRMAN: And now, ladies and gentlemen, at last, I should like to
   welcome to our little - music-hall - one or two of the worthier burghers -
   yes, burghers is what I said, madam; your hearing rather than my diction
   is at fault if you think I said anything else - of this most noble borough
   . . . I notice, among them, our gallant upholder of the law, taking a well-
   earned rest from the chase of the elusive Mary Ann - Chief Constable
   Jackson!

   (JACKSON rises and acknowledges applause. As he does so, four
   ENTERTAINERS in policemens uniforms appear on the stage and sing
   'The Bold Gendarmes.)

ENTERTAINERS: We're public guardians, bold, yet wary.
   And of ourselves we take good care.
   To risk our precious lives we're chary,
   When danger looms we're never there.
   But when we meet a helpless woman,
   Or little boys that do no harm,
   We run them in,
   We show them we're the bold gendarmes,
   We run them in (etc).

   Sometimes our duty's extramural,
   Then little butterflies we chase,
   We like to gambol in things rural,
   Commune with nature face to face,
   Unto our beat then back returning,
   Refreshed by Nature's holy charms.
   We run them in,
   We show them we're the bold gendarmes.
   We run them in (etc).

(The number concludes and the ENTERTAINERS go off amid applause.)

CHAIRMAN: He runs them in indeed . . . Now over there I see another of our distinguished citizens - the veritable Asmoday of our times - the man who takes the lids off our lives and sells them back to us next day at a penny a copy; our fearless and outspoken leader of the press - Mr William Leng!

(LENG rises to a mixed reaction.)

- And again, over there, if I'm not very much mistaken -

(As the CHAIRMAN is about to introduce another guest, BROADHEAD enters and is spotted by the CHAIRMAN.)

But no, one moment, ladies and gentlemen! Whom have we here? Here to complete this evening's plethora of celebrity? Allow me to present -

OLD MAN: It's Owd Smeetem hisself!

FIRST WOMAN: What's up? Come to collect were natty, have you?

SECOND WORKMAN: Or have you come to blow us all up?

(Rowdy applause, jeers and cheers. One or two start to chant 'Mary Ann, Mary Ann . . .'.)

WOMAN (over the hubbub): He's done more for t' working man than any of you bloody lot!

CHAIRMAN (banging his gavel): Order, please, order, ladies and gentlemen - ladies, please.

FIRST WORKMAN: Speak for theeself.

CHAIRMAN: With your permission, I suggest we invite Mr Broadhead to come forward and tell us -

BROADHEAD: No, no. I haven't come here to make a speech.

MAN: Let's hear him!

OLD MAN: Aye, let's hear Owd Smeetem!

(Chant of 'Speech, speech'.)

CHAIRMAN: It's no use, Mr Broadhead. We will not allow you to escape without hearing a few of your well-chosen phrases . . . please.

(Renewed applause, mostly ironical.)

FIRST WORKMAN: Has tha nowt to say for thyself?

SECOND WORKMAN: Tha were never slow at making speeches a while back. Cat got thy tongue?

THIRD WORKMAN: Give 'im a chance.

(BROADHEAD is urged to the front. The noise subsides.)

BROADHEAD: I haven't come here to create a disturbance, or to make a speech. I hoped I would not be noticed at all. But there are just one or two things I'd like you to know before I leave Sheffield for good.

FIRST WORKMAN: Good riddance.

CHAIRMAN: Silence, please.

(Cries of 'Hooray', 'Good riddance', and 'Shut up, let's hear him talk'.)

BROADHEAD: I don't want anybody to think I'm offering excuses for what I've done in the past. I'm just as liable to make mistakes as anybody else. But through all the howlings, the clamour and the threats with which I've been hunted down, I've had this consolation, that my only wish and object has been to protect and defend the labour of thousands of work-men.

THIRD WORKMAN: That's reet.

(A few genuine cheers.)

BROADHEAD: I've always striven to do this to the best of my humble ability. If others had been more honest and their motives as pure as mine, the sins I've been condemned for would never have been committed.

THIRD WORKMAN: True enough.

BROADHEAD: My worst deeds are publicly known, which is more than can be said for many of those who have howled against me with such assumed virtue. If they had been in the same circumstances, perhaps they wouldn't have done much better. What I've done has been for the good of others and not for the benefit of myself. The error of my life has been that I have loved the trade unions not wisely, but too well.

SECOND WORKMAN: Well said Mr Broadhead.

BROADHEAD: With the help of loyal friends - and I still have friends - I intend for the sake of my family to attempt to start a new life in America, but I know that to the end of my days, whatever my fellow citizens think of me, I shall always feel a very lively interest in the welfare and the future prosperity of the good old town of Sheffield.

(His small group of supporters vigorously clap.)

THIRD WORKMAN: Good Old Mary Ann.

(BROADHEAD steps down.)

SECOND WORKMAN: Aye, goodbye, Mary Ann!

(The GIRL SINGERS in police uniform take this as a cue.)

GIRL SINGERS: 'Yes, I always will be true to Mary Ann, Mary Ann!

(Laughter and applause. They continue.)

'I always will be true to Mary Hann;
Let others wander far, I'm happier as I are,
And I always will be true to Mary Hann . . .'

We members of the force, as a matter quite o' course,
Takes the smiles and the advances of the fair;
But some of us, is true to Sarah, Jane, or Sue,
Though such hinstances, of course, are rather rare;
For my hown part all I'll say, is I never wish to stray

Or hinterfere with hany hother man;
Contented with my lot, I stick to what I've got -
And I halways will be true to Mary Hann!
Yes I always will be true to Mary Hann!
Yes I always will be true to Mary Ann, Mary Ann -
I always will be true to Mary Ann:
Let others wander far, I'm happier as I are,
And I always will be true to Mary Ann.

(All dance off stage, leaving BROADHEAD.)

LENG: Mr Broadhead, may I wish you bon voyage?

BROADHEAD: Thank you.

LENG: There was never anything personal, you know.

BROADHEAD: You did what you had to do.

LENG: Just as you had nothing personal against Linley.

BROADHEAD: I did what I had to do.

(A NEWSBOY crosses, shouting 'New Charter for the Workers. Trade Union Bill passed in Parliament'.)

LENG: Perhaps we have both done what we set out to do.

BROADHEAD: Goodbye, Mr Leng.

(They raise their hats to each other. LENG exits. The GIRL SINGERS lead the company on.)

GIRL SINGERS: Ye Muses who mount on Parnassian towers,
Come trooping to Sheffield and help me to sing
The time when our sons have all got out their sours,
And relate all the joys that our Saturdays bring.

BROADHEAD: But hard words and Greek-em
                Let learned folk speak 'em;
It's epic and tragic, bombastic we'll write:

ALL: And loudly we'll sing-o
                In plain English lingo
The stirrings in Sheffield on Saturday night.

The Stirrings in Sheffield

Ye Muses who mount on Par-nas-si-an towers come trooping to Sheffield and help me to sing — The time when our sons have all got out their sours. And re-late all the joys that out Sat-ur-days bring. But hard words and Greek'em, let learned folks speak'em its epic and tra-gic bom-bas-tic we'll write — And loud-ly we'll sing-o in plain English lingo the Stirrings in Sheffield on Sat-ur-day night.

Grinder's Hardships

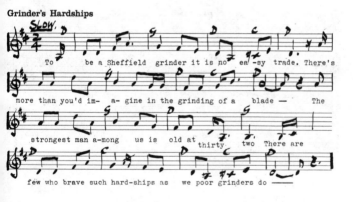

To be a Sheffield grinder it is no ea-sy trade. There's more than you'd im-a-gine in the grinding of a blade — The strongest man a-mong us is old at thirty two There are few who brave such hard-ships as we poor grinders do ——

Gas Song

Tho' coal was cheap in Sheffield, And labour costs were small, The
price of gas was twice as much as anywhere else at all.
Ah Pro-gress! This fa-vour we en-treat, Get
beau-ti-ful big gas-ome-ters built in ev'ry Sheffield street.

Last chorus, repeat from *

-ometers built in ev'ry Sheffield, street, oy!
ev'ry
Sheffield

Sheffield Workmen

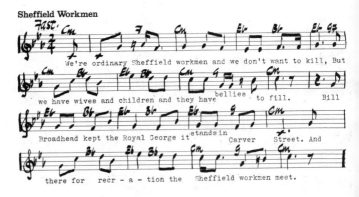

We're ordinary Sheffield workmen and we don't want to kill, But
we have wives and children and they have bellies to fill. Bill
Broadhead kept the Royal George it stands in Carver Street. And
there for recr - a - tion the Sheffield workmen meet.

Collier Lass

sung unacc. in free speech rhythm.

My name is Polly Parker, I've come o'er from Barnsley. My father and mother work in the coal mine. Our fam-i-ly's large, we have got se-ven children, so I am o-blig'd to work in the same mine. But as this is my fortune, I know you'll be sorry, that in such em-ploy-ment my days I must pass. But to keep up my spirits I sing and look merry, Al--though I am on-ly a poor coll-ier lass.

Thomas Paine & We've Been Sent

God Save great Thom-as Paine. His Rights of Man t'explain, To ev-ery Soul————. He makes the blind to see

We've been sent to Sheffield Town————. Sent to keep the workers down.

What dupes and slaves they be, And points out

We've been sent to Sheffield Town. They made a fuss of us when we got there.

Li- ber-ty from———— pole to pole.

met us with a band in Paradise Square. We've been sent to Sheffield Town.

St Patrick

St Pat-rick was a gen-tle man. He came of de—cent peo-ple. He built a church in Dub-lin Town, and on it put a stee—ple.

I'm Ruined

I'm ruined, I'm ruined but I can't com-plain. My ruin, my ruin has not been in vain. For me dia-monds and pearls and me place in Park Lane. I'd be Ru- hu- hu-in'd all o-ver a- gain.

Mary Anne

We members of the force, as a matter quite of course, takes the smiles and the ad-van-ces of the fair—. But some of us is true, to Sar-ah, Jane or Sue. Tho' such in-stan-ces of course are rather rare. For my own part all I'll say is, I ne-ver wish to stray. Or in-ter-fere with any oth-er man—. Con-tent'd with my lot, I'll stick to what I've got and I always will be true to Mary Anne. Yes I always will be true to Mary Anne, Mary Anne. I al-ways will be true to Mary Anne. Let others wander far, I'm happier as I are, And I al-ways will be true to Mary Anne—.

METHUEN PLAYSCRIPTS

*If you would like regular information
on new Methuen plays, please write to*
The Marketing Department
Eyre Methuen Ltd
11 New Fetter Lane
London EC4P 4EE